Alladi
Magical Memoir

by
Alladin Kamria

Foreword & Edited by Zurain Imam (Karachi Pakistan)

The desire and dedication to pen one's memoirs in the autumn of one's life - one filled with upheavals, struggles, adventures, and success- requires great courage; fortitude; a perennially youthful (and mischievous) spirit and a kind heart. These qualities are the very reason why I was delighted and agreed to help Alladin Kamria — known to me as Ali Uncle-edit his multi- volume reminisces of his eventful life. Ali Uncle is family to me. In the roaring late '50s he was "adopted" by the Imam brothers - my paternal uncles- when he met them in Karachi and developed a specially close relationship with my father, M. Zaffar Imam (Late).

There are countless sepia photographs in our family archives of the two of them frolicking and dancing at nightclubs with glamorous women or posing casually at the beach and other locales. This first volume (Vol. 1) of "Alladin's Magical Memoirs" recounts the memoirist's early years growing up in Bombay with an intimate introduction to his family and relationships with school friends and work colleagues; some of which have been sustained for over 60 years; the young and ambitious teenager working at his father's restaurant; squabbles with school bullies; finding professional independence working at a factory; catching the infectious acting bug and performing on stage and on-screen and of course his myriad love affairs and breaking of hearts including a tribute to "the love of his life."

In a Simple stream of consciousness writing style, Alladin Kamria poignantly recollects his earliest memories which formed the genesis and foundation of the gentleman he has become, one who has still kept his "naughty" inner child indubitably alive.

Front cover design – By my son-in-law Dan Beers

Volume 1

I was six years old and playing in the woods with my friends. It was getting dark and gloomy. Ominous clouds were gradually approaching with a sudden storm burst of lightning and thunder. Scared and desperately fearful, I turned around to garner some comfort but to my horror they had mysteriously vanished, and I was left alone, now more scared than ever. I cried out to God and was answered with another resounding bout of thunder and lightning.

This time the lightning stuck the ground not far from me and in its glorious light I saw an opening to a cave, to which I ran towards as fast as my little legs could carry me. I thanked God profusely with chattering teeth with the drenched clothes and fear taking its toll. As if I was not suffering enough from fear, I heard a deafening ear-splitting sound from behind me. My heart stopped as I reluctantly turned and saw a big boulder hurtling towards me as I froze.

I mustered enough courage and ran fast, and suddenly felt someone shaking me gently to wake up as if I was dreaming. It was my darling granny, "My son you were dreaming", she explained to me gently. I groaned a sigh of relief still shuddering from the harrowing experience. You might imagine that I was influenced by the Indiana Jones movies, but it was 1944 and the movie was made in 1981 by Hollywood. But, that day onwards, I have always wondered about the genesis and formation of dreams and from where the emanate deep in one's inner consciousness.

As a young boy, I used to watch my granny take a small bowl of cold water and pour 4711 eau de cologne into it and then dip strips of cloth into the mixture. She would then squeeze the dampness from the cloth and place it on the fevered forehead. She would keep replacing the warm cloth with the fresh cold ones until fever subsided. This loving regime was in lieu of antibiotics. Growing up, our family never took antibiotics and thankfully always remained healthy.

My granny's healing regimen is an example of the kind patience, love and protective nurturing my siblings and I received from both our granny and my mum, who sacrificed her life for her eight children, my father and her own mum, my granny. I have always maintained that no one, absolutely no one can take the place of one's mother. Muslims believe that heaven indubitably lies the beneath the feet of our mothers.

Once a faithful approached the Prophet Muhammad (Peace Be Upon Him) and asked, "Oh, Messenger of God, who should I spend my time most with and love?" The holy Prophet replied "Your Mother". The faithful asked the same question three times and got the same reply. Upon the fourth questioning, the Holy Prophet replied,

"Your father." In other words, one's mother receives the gold, silver, and bronze medals while one's father gamers a consolation prize.

My father was the single bread winner and was responsible for feeding and clothing all of us, while each of us shared in the daily household chores.

My father came to Bombay India in 1924 from Sirjan in the province of Kerman Iran, while my mother hails from Shahrbabak, also from the same province of Kerman. They got married in 1926 and had eight children.

The first born arrived in 1928 my father named her Nosrat – the second girl was named Heshmat – the third son Ghulam Hussein – the fourth girl Meher Sultan - I am the fifth, and was named Alladin (and not Aladdin as portrayed in movies and fairy tales)- the sixth son Saifudin – the seventh son Farrokh, and the last one girl Umeh Habibeh. When Nosrat and Hesbmat were older

Aga Khan the third named her Firouze and Prince Ali Khan named Heshmat Bibi Tela.

All the sisters were pretty but Firouze and Meher were truly stunning. The brothers were also all handsome and everyone in our compound called us "the valiant brothers." Not to seem narcissistic, but I was considered the most handsome although I believed my older brother Ghulam Hussein was more so.

Ghulam Hussein was not very inclined towards education and wanted to become a jockey in thoroughbred racing, encouraged by my uncle Ali Khan, who was a trainer and owner of thoroughbred horses. Uncle Ali Khan arranged for my enthusiastic brother to enrol at the jockey apprentice school in Calcutta run by an Anglo-Indian retired Major who was a great rider and teacher. Those who completed their five years of apprenticeship turned out to be accomplished race jockeys.

My uncle had a string of 30 horses out of which he owned 10 and the rest he trained for different owners. He had hoped to get Ghulam Hussein under his wings. Unfortunately, he was not a trainer anymore. Any day when his horses would enter to run in a race, my uncle would sleep in the stables to make sure that no one, out of enmity, would tamper with them.

Tap Dance, a big chestnut stallion, was to run in a race and my uncle instinctively felt his win a sure thing. The night before the races, due to unforeseen circumstances, he could not sleep in the barn, and his foreman received a bribe from his enemy to drug Tap Dance. The foreman injected Tap Dance with doping drugs and Tap Dance won the race by ten lengths. The Stewards checked the swab and sure enough the swab came positive. Sadly, my uncle lost his license. This was also a big blow for my brother as he was counting to join my uncle after his apprenticeship.

Fortunately, my brother-in-law Akbar Khan was also a trainer with few horses, and he took my brother under his wing. Akbar Khan had a mare named Georgette, though ten years old competed with younger horses, and even won two races with my brother Ghulam Hussein as her jockey.

After a while my brother began putting on weight - disastrous for a jockey and in spite of his myriad efforts he could not lose the extraneous pounds. He finally gave up and could not ride again. No trainers were giving him any rides and for a while he became a riding boy - riding horses early mornings to exercise them - finally he gave up that too.

How my father arrived in Bombay is in itself a sure-fire example of great will, courage, and persistence. His family in Iran were all poor and worked as pickers in pistachio fields which my father also partook in from the age of six. He saved every penny to fulfil his dreams of going to Bombay, about which he had heard of plenty of success stories. Almost all Iranians who emigrated to India eventually opened Ionian restaurants or bakeries: a trend which still holds true till today.

One fine day, my father packed all his clothes, comprising two pairs of pants and shirts, and embarked on the indubitable arduous journey. He received the blessing of his parents and started to walk from Sirjan to Bunder Abbas, which was a seaport over 305 miles away. He was tough and had the will and confidence; walking and hitching rides on camels or donkeys. It took him under a month to reach Bunder Abbas where he finally boarded a freight ship on whose deck he worked and slept. At the tender age of 16, this was his first time away from home and the first time on a voyage.

When he finally arrived at the Bombay sea port of Mazgaon Dock,s he was overwhelmed by all the hustle and bustle. The motley crowd made from a mixture of Indians in their divergent garbs;

Englishmen dressed in their half pants, shirts and sun hats; lorries being loaded with imported goods drove to the godowns -warehouses. Long carts on two wheels were also loaded which poor Indians young and old pulled and tugged their torn shirts drenched with sweat. They toiled and moiled. They toiled and moiled earning enough, to feed their families. Till today it exists.

All of this cosmopolitan frenzy was too much to absorb for a village boy who was dumbfounded, panic stricken and fearful. He cried aloud "Oh my God how am I going to survive! I don't even speak any language except Farsi" my young father prayed to God: "In THEE I put my trust and through patience and prayers I seek YOUR help."

My father had thirty Indian Rupees, which in those days was worth a little more than a British Pound. India was under British Raj, so all currencies were pegged to the Pounds. On the ship, my father had met an Iranian gentleman who could speak

English. He took my father to his destination: Aga Hall, Nesbit Road, Mazagon Bombay.

My father felt fortunate and elated to be among Iranians who were the major residents of this very big compound. Having settled down, his first job was selling Pashmak an Iranian sweet treat, similar to cotton candy (but way better in taste and texture). He used to wake up early at three in the morning to go to the bakery and collect a large, round aluminium pot of Pashmak with which he would walk around from one Iranian retailer to another till three in the afternoon when he returned totally exhausted.

Apart from selling Pashmak, my father was the night watchman for Aga Khan, the Third Sultan Mohammad Shah, whose room he sat right outside of till morning. He received a few Rupees per month from the respected Lady Ali Shah, mother of the Aga Khan. My father was well-versed in Arabic and Farsi so he used to perform the funeral prayers and rites for the deceased followers of the Aga Khan. From the 1930s to the 1950s, my father also performed Nikah (Muslim marital prayers to join couples in holy matrimony according to Muslim laws). For this free loyal services to the community, the Aga Khan later bestowed on him the title of "Alijah" denoting a high place.

Having come from a poor background my father had learned at a very early age the value of money for he had to work hard for pennies, and it was no different now. He saved every penny and as the old saying goes - you take care of the pennies and the pounds will take care of themselves.

After a couple of years he had saved enough to acquire a five feet by five feet place, where he placed a small table, a large Samovar - a decorated tea - filled with tea which has always been popular in India because they knew the exact proportions of tea leaves, water, milk and sugar to be added to the Samovar. My father also placed two large glass jars filled with 'bisquits', Hindi for what one calls cookies in America, as well as cakes and buns spread on a large tray.

My entrepreneurial father was an early riser, who would wake up by four in the morning, who would then walk to the Iranian bakery to collect the 'bisquits', buns, and cakes on credit (as the bakery knew my father from his Pashmak days); opening shop by five thirty and ready for his customers.

His customers were also poor people so they did not mind standing on the footpath and sipping the piping hot tea with cakes or buns.

While my dad was the only bread winner, everyone else in the household helped in any way they could, the eldest with more chores than the others and the youngest with less. The eldest sister Firouze performed most of the chores helping my mum. My youngest brothers, Saifudin and Farrokh, and sister Umeh Habibeh, enjoyed themselves doing nothing but playing in the compound.

I was six, and along with my brother Ghulam Hussein, had to help out in the very first restaurant my father had bought - Atlas restaurant. After returning from school four in the afternoon, we had tea, then took our books and went walking about five miles to the restaurant. We wished our dad and started working.

The only thing we had to do was pick up the dishes after the customers had finished eating and take it to the bus boy and clean tables for the customers. After a couple of hours, we used to take a break and go and play with the kids for a while before returning back to work till ten in the night. After ten our tutor came and taught us to complete our homework till eleven closing time.

We walked back home with our dad and by the time we reached home it would be close to midnight, once home we would take a cold bath and go to sleep. The next day followed the same routine. After a while, there was a feeling that our father was taking too much out of us. In later years when I ventured on my own, I realised all the hard work stood in good stead, and it was then that I was thankful to my dad.

My mum had two brothers, Sohrab Khan who was mostly in Madras and Bangalore, and was a trainer and owner of thoroughbred horses. My younger uncle Ali Khan was also in the same field, but he lived in Bombay and Poona. They loved us like their own children as both remained bachelors their entire lives. My uncle Ali Khan used to come and visit my dad in the restaurant. We used to plead with him to ask our dad to allow us to go home with him. He had contracted a horse carriage on a monthly basis called Victoria named after the Queen. My father could never refuse him and we rode back extremely happy.

Daily business was picking up and more and more people began coming not only for breakfast but for lunch because my father had added boiled eggs and 'pao roti'(Hindi for square breads). He would make sandwiches by spreading some butter on the bread and then adding boiled eggs, salt and black pepper which became a favourite of the customers.

My father's savings started piling up faster than he had expected and within two years he was able to open a small full-fledged Iranian restaurant. He furnished it with about seven tables and accompanying chairs and from the get-go all the tables would be filled for breakfast, lunch and dinner. The latter two meals included three different curries on the menu which the 'table walla' (Hindi for waiter) would suggest to each customer as there was no paper menu. The waiter would recommend "specialties", even though the curries were pretty much the same.

The restaurant was a couple of miles from our home. My father was the first to arrive at four in the morning and the last to leave at around 12 midnight.

Typically, he would go to the bazaars to buy produce for the restaurant, so that by the time the restaurant staff and cook arrived they had everything at their disposal to begin cooking and serving.

His hard work and good habit of saving was paying off so after a few years he sold his restaurant and bought a better one in Kala Ghoda, and simultaneously a smaller one in Dongri which was not as good of an area. It was named Gulzar Persian Restaurant. Soon, he sold the Kala Ghoda restaurant at a good price and bought a small one in Null Bazar and a cold drink house named "G.R. Vafadari" in Golpitah, G.R. being the initials of my father for Ghulam Reza. Here, all kind of sodas and sherbets were served.

A little bit further on, he bought one opposite Alankar Cinema house named Bharat Café, which was the only one left at the time of his death.

My father had heard about success stories when he was a kid in Sirjan and now he had worked on his inspiration and followed his goals and succeeded with determination, lots of hard work, patience, and courage (which is the most important of all the qualities he had). Without courage, he could not have fulfilled his dreams. In all senses of the words, he was a self-made man. May he rest in peace.

Aga Hall was built by Aga Khan the first. With his family and loyal followers from Iran and their families, Imam Hassan Ali Shah emigrated from Iran down to Bombay via Sindh and Poona. The entrance to the Aga Khan palace had six wide marble steps, leading to a long rectangular marble verandah which was about 20x15 feet wide and was surrounded by decorative cast iron rails similar to those in the French Quarter in New Orleans.

The verandah was one of the biggest blessings for myself and all my friends who used to go to sleep there our bedding consisted of a beach mat; a pillow and one bed sheet for covering. Boys being boys, we would stay up chatting and joking about girls till we fell asleep.

During the monsoon season, we endured four months of rain amounting to about 100 inches and rendering the weather extremely humid and warm. Thunder and lightning were also often experienced during monsoon nights, which lit up the verandah where there was no protection in the sides. The verandah was covered, as it was directly under the palace's floor, but the sides were just decorative cast iron.

When it rained, it was accompanied with a strong wind blowing towards us with the end result that part of our bedding became wet. Many a times the lightening was so intense, striking the ground 25 feet from us to which we would exclaim "Glory be to God!" All of us had actually gotten used to the tumultuous weather and actually enjoyed it and were not scared. These experiences have left an indelible print on my brain even till now; indubitably great memories few get to experience.

The inside compound measured about seven acres and was peopled by around 100 families in houses small, medium and large. Needless to say the larger houses were given to the Aga Khan's close and distant relatives, while family like ours got the medium-sized house. My grandmother worked for lady Ali Shah, the wife of Aga Khan the second and mother of the Aga Khan the third Sultan Mohammad Shah but sadly, she was given the smallest house.

The palace had spacious beautiful lawns on all three sides; the one facing it was about 300 feet long; the one facing our house was about 150 feet long and the one which faced the left of the palace was about 250 feet long. All three lawns were about 35 feet wide and really resembled gems in a jewelled plain. The left and the right lawns had fountains in the centre.

Facing the palace right in the centre was a really large fountain surrounded by marble seats. Old and young, rich and poor gathered every night discussing current affairs. The fountain housed an expansive pond filled with fish whose scales glimmered in the moonlight. In this respect we were lucky to have been born in this bucolic and idyllic place.

The calming and soothing sounds of water from the fountain is a childhood memory I will never forget. Water is and indispensable element of the Islamic Garden. Add to its vista, blue skies which radiated all year round in Bombay except during the monsoon season, with lush greenery; all of this lent a sense of serenity and peace.

Looking at the morning dew on the flower petals and on the grass was a spiritual experience in itself. My grandmother who was an early riser would meditate at 4 am for an hour of deep slow inner breathing while taking the name of Allah and slowly breathing out. She always walked on the wet grass and exclaimed "Oh Allah every dew drop praises Your splendour for there is no might and power greater than YOU!" She used to say the lush green hues of the grass lit up as soon as the sun rose and resembled emerald green.

To experience this bliss and joy she advised me to rise early and praise God. In the domain of spirituality my granny was considered pious and holy and I myself showed an interest in spirituality from the early age of six. I owe all my spiritual nature to her. She taught me what is morally right and wrong, and taught me how to pray. She told my life is not all about playing, eating and sleeping, but that one will face trials and tribulations all through one's life.

My granny further advised me that in times of distress, one must take refuge with God. One must learn to sit in solitude and contemplate on HIM and one will undoubtedly find spiritual serenity.

One will experience this perfect peace and happiness by meditating every day, beginning with a few minutes and gradually reaching a state of spiritual bliss. A further Me guideline from granny to me was always remember to maintain a balance between the spiritual and material, and not to rush as I had my whole life ahead of me.

The compound was lined with tropical trees including Tamarind, Chickoo, Amla, Guava, Jamun (both white and purple), Papaya, Mango and Tardgola (ice apple in English) which was luscious. Last but not the least, there were some tiny sweet, mouth-watering berries with seeds, which we grabbed in handfuls and filled our pockets with to take them to school. We were about six or seven years old, small and agile, and be able to climb the mango trees like monkeys; pluck green raw mangoes called kairi and hurl them to the ground and devour them with salt and chili powder.

We did the same with Tamarinds which had greenish-brown colour and were quite crisp and also on the sour side and again delicious with the above-mentioned seasonings. There was also an Almond tree from which we picked when it was half ripe. We would crack the shell with stone and enjoy the tasty almond seed.

Thank God we were born to live in this, heavenly place with its, beauty and magnificent splendor which today seems like a dream; gone and never to be experienced again alas, not even in my dreams yet...

We had plenty of space between lawns to play various games among ourselves including football (America is the only country calls it soccer) which originated in England around 1665 and cricket. Also, great Indian games like Kabaddi a team sport on a small field between two teams on opposite halves of the field. They take turn sending a "raider" into the other half. This is to win points by tackling, in one breath members of the opposing team. We also played Atya Patya (game of feints) for which all you needed was chalk powder to draw lines and you were good to go.

As Bombay was humid all year round, we used to sweat profusely. After we finished playing, we quenched our thirst with God's natural spring water which was relatively cold compared to the outdoor temperature. The palace's main entrance which had marble steps also had an alternative left-side entrance; wrought iron spiral steps which led straight up to the top floor of the palace.

The miraculous spring water fountain was located to the left side of the iron steps among completely dry grounds. These steps led straight to the palace and was often used by the Palace librarian, Qassam who looked after a huge collection of books ranging from great Persian scholars like Hafez, Saadi, Omar Khayyam among others. The library also boasted a stunning collection of Shakespeare's plays; Charles Dickens' novels; John Milton and volumes of great philosophers like Plato and Aristotle.

Since Qassam was in charge of the library, he had plenty of extra time which he used to help the elderly who lived in the compound with all kinds of work outside the compound which they could not leave and hence could not do their own. In those days most compound dwellers did not own cars and only a few, if any owned bicycles.

The most common mode of transport for almost all citizens of Bombay was either the tram or the double-decker bus. Everybody both large or small, ran along the fast-moving tram and just jumped on to board it. One sad day we received the horrifying news that Qassam while trying to jump on to the tram fell and one of his legs went under the tram's rails. He was rushed to the hospital and the doctors had no choice but to amputate his leg. For the rest of his life he used crutches as he did not opt for any prosthetics. Qassam passed away around ten years after his accident and he was always missed.

To the extreme left side of the palace there was a big house which belonged to Najafi Aunty, who had five children; three girls and two boys; Zeenat, Ezzat, Nosrat; Amman and Charlie. Next to this family's home there was a string of three houses. These were occupied by Noorie Uncle, Hashem Khan who we called Archie Baba and next to them was occupied by Kaiser Ahmed, his wife Pussy Aunty and their daughters Humayoun, Rezwan,[and Farhat. The next and last house was occupied by uncle Sheikh Abbas; his wife Gulshan Nanni and their daughter Saffiyeh.

Najafi Aunty's daughter Nosrat was my first true love and remains thus till today, Nosrat's sister Ezzat was like my own loving sister. Najafi aunty did not approve of the pairing of Nosrat and myself as she had plans for her daughter to wed someone rich as my family was not rich and middle class. But as far as esteem was concerned, my father was one of the most well- respected man living in the compound along with Hashem Khan and Kaiser Ahmed who were both down-to-earth though they were well placed in life.

Hashem Khan was very close to my uncle Ali Khan and they were inseparable, like brothers usually playing cards with friends. Evenings were reserved for drinking with appetizers like roasted spiced peanuts and kababs.

Mehdi and Hadi, Hashem Khan's nephews lived with him because their Cambridge Section of St. Mary school was walking distance from our compound. It was more expensive than St. Mary English section, which I attended, and both schools were situated across the street from each other.

Mehdi and Hadi were very close friends of mine. Mehdi was a bit of a friendly bully whereas Hadi was quite the opposite. They used to take me to their mom's house Gowhar Aunty for lunch in Colaba, a posh area of Bombay. With both her arms graced with gold and glass bangles and canvassed with heavy makeup, she also enjoyed drinking. She was a classy lady and I always thought she looked like Hollywood actress Rosalind Russell.

Mehdi and Hadi were from a good, high clan family but they never aired their status with the compound people. They were, intead, polite. They, of course, did not socialize with anyone, but they played games with us. They knew their uncle Hahem was a very close friend of our family, and we were the only ones who could visit their house along with Sheikh Abbas, and Pussy Aunty's house.

Hadi had a cute white sheep dog who he loved a lot. One day we were playing, cricket and Noorie uncle raced his car in the compound. We simultaneously heard the loud howling of Hadi's dog. Our hearts sank and both Hadi and I were in tears as we found the dog lying next to the car. Hadi was petting the dog gently who was seriously wounded. We both knew he would soon pass away and sure enough the poor dog whimpered his last breath. Noorie Uncle's face was flushed full of guilt and repentance and he repeatedly continued to apologize to Hadi.

Mehdi was much older than me and he oftentimes displayed brotherly love towards me. One of my most memorable incidents was when Mehdi took me to his school, where the student's roller- skated. He got me a pair of skates and taught me how to skate and after skating we went to the canteen where some chocolates were right in the front row. My eyes fell on Mars bar which I always craved but could never afford. Mehdi asked me which one I wanted, and I reluctantly asked to have the Mars bar and Mehdi immediately bought it for me. That was the first time I felt that little things like that left indelible, everlasting, and life-long memories.

Psychically as I was reminiscing and penning my good memories about Mehdi, Hashem Khan's daughter Qamar Mehdi's cousin texted me with the sad news that Mehdi had passed away. It was extremely difficult to digest this sad news. May God bless his kind soul.

Hadi is still alive and well by the grace of God and I called him in Bombay offering him my heartfelt condolence on his great loss and we fondly reminisced about our great times together.

Gulshan Nani loved me and knew all my secrets. I was in Pussy Aunty's house at least two or three times a week and from there I made it a point to visit Gulshan Nani, who really loved me. She used to spoil me with tea and cakes, and I used to share all my secrets with her. She was truly my confidant. After she had listened to stories of my escapades, she would say in Farsi - "Felfel nabin chi reeze bekhor bebin chi teeze" (chili might be tiny but if you eat it you feel how hot it is).

Pussy Aunty very much resembled Hollywood star Susan Hayward and I considered her even more beautiful than Hayward. All the ladies in the compound were pretty. First and foremost was Pussy Aunty, then Doris Aunty, the mother of my childhood friend Aziz. Doris was a distant relative of the Aga Khan, and a very loving person who the whole compound loved and respected.

From Pussy Aunty's three girls, the eldest Humayoun, in later years developed kidney disease and finally succumbed to her ailment. Rezwan resides in Poona, India and Farhat who always calls me bhaijaan (beloved brother) lives in Toronto, Canada with her good husband Mehboob, another friendly chap. We occasionally speak now and then, reminiscing about the good old days in the compound.

Hashem Khan's wife, Dolly Aunty was a very pretty woman both inside and out and was like a sister to my sister Bibi Tela. She had six children all sweet like their mother, good looking inside and out. Qamar, Qassam, Yasmin, Mehjabin, Firdows, and Aslam. I am blessed to still be in contact with all of them. I am much older than all of them and consider them my brothers and sisters.

Behind the compound houses were three mouses. The first belonged to Hussein Shaharbabaki who came from Iran the same time my father arrived in India. He and his wife had five children, Rajab, Nizar, Farideh, Noordin, and Mahvesh. We were good friends and played together as I have already mentioned earlier. It was Rajab and I who wanted to have a sports team of our own in the compound. Wanting is one thing but to make it a reality, is practically impossible due to lack of funds. Nobody in the compound was that rich and those who had the money kind of laughed at our ambitious idea.

The second house belonged to Qassam the librarian, and the third to Gulandoon, an African-Iranian woman. Her parents had settled down in Bombay. The games we played in the compound with the exception of cricket and football, we did not need any sports equipment; games which I have described earlier including gilli dandi, atiya patiya, sticks and stones etc.

After playing games Rajab and 1 would rack our brains to come up with ideas to raise money. As they say when there is a will there is a way. With our goal in mind, we came up with a simple yet great solution. Rajab worked at a printing press he was older than me and as soon as he graduated from high school, he went to work, while we were still in school. He printed receipt books which resembled check books. I, the bold one with a gift of the gab, went out and convinced the well to do in the compound and even from outside to help us.

It took us about two months, and I collected enough to buy all the equipment for cricket, including two bats, gloves for a wicket keeper, six stumps the whole works. Football was a less expensive affair, all that was needed were two footballs and no need of special boots as we played in our canvas shoes.

Obviously, the name of the club became the Aga Khan Sports club and soon we began playing watches with other teams and we became really very good. Rajab captained the team and I was the vice-captain, our treasurer was Tajudin, an alcoholic who had a few days being sober but who nevertheless was loved by everybody. I don't know what came over us to appoint him, but we could not fire him. When funds for replacing old equipment were diminished and there was money in the kitty and despite all the setbacks we kept on winning matches and generous citizens were glad to help again.

The team comprised of 15 to 17 years old. I was 15 and always played the wicketkeeper not speaking in adulation but I was pretty damn good, as a batsman I was okay and usually went fifth to bat and the highest I scored was 82 runs. We had good bowlers both fast and slow who usually spun the ball in off or leg break and sometimes a googly. The batsman could not figure out whether the ball was going to land off or leg break. This was done to confuse the batsman and most of the time the wicket would fall, and the batsman was out.

Koloo, our Iranian friend from the compound, was getting married and we wanted to arrange some entertainment. He although poor was a jovial fellow who made everybody laugh and had a good singing voice similar to Saigal, an older famous Indian singer. I gathered all the kids together to brainstorm and plan how to arrange a Qawaali night. The genie was originally an Islamic-Sufi from of devotional music and poetry. Later on ghazals and gets were added to the music spectrum. Qawaali became very popular and today is one of the most popular forms of entertainment for occasions like weddings and birthdays.

Koloo our Iranian friend from the compound was getting married and we wanted to arrange some entertainment, who although poor, was a jovial fellow who made everybody laugh and had a good singing voice similar to Saigal an older famous singer.

I gathered all the kids to brainstorm and plan to arrange a Qawwali night. This genre was originally an Islamic—Sufi form of devotional music and poetry. Later on, ghazals and geets were added to the music spectrum.

Qawwali became very popular forms of entertainment for occasions of weddings and birthdays.

I had heard about a very young Qawwal, about our age named Aziz Naza Qawwal who we thought, would be easy to get to perform for us. We were all still in school and all our pocket money combined would not be enough to hire Aziz Naza for the night. One of the restaurants that my father owned was Gulzar Persian Restaurant in Dongri, which was very close to Aziz Naza's house. Later after a few years when he became very popular, he rented a room right above our restaurant, which he converted to his music room.

I was already known for collecting funds and approached everyone in the compound to chip in. I collected about Rupees 140 and during a visit to my father's restaurant, I waited for Aziz to come down, and asked him about our Qawwali evening. Although he was not yet famous, he nevertheless acted as if he were a top star. He told me that his charges were Rupees 75 and he would require an advance of Rupees 25. He further cautioned that if for any reason we cancelled, the advance would not be returned.

He further cautioned us that if for any reason we cancelled, the advance would not be returned.

Koloo was getting married to a Khoja girl who was very kind, sincere and a good person. After the religious wedding ceremony, all the compound guests got together singing Iranian congratulatory wedding songs. One of them played the Daereh', a kind of a round handheld drum while circling the big fountain. In the midst of the singing, someone came running towards us screaming to please stop the celebrations as Sheikh Abbas had passed away. Everybody respected the recently departed and immediately stopped all the festivities. My first reaction was to run to Gulshan Nani to offer my condolence. She was someone who showed me love and we sat together crying.

It was around five in the afternoon and Mahmood and I rushed to Aziz Naza to cancel the

Qawaali program which was to take place later that night. Aziz insisted that he would not return the advance, and that we would have to pay him the remaining fee and he reasoned that he could have taken up another program. I pleaded with him, telling him we were neighbours and about my father and his restaurant where he and his friends enjoyed tea together. He finally accepted to only keep the advance, and when we would decide on a future date, he would only take the balance.

After six weeks, I approached Aziz to set a new date. By now he had become a friend. After the cancellation, whenever I visited my dad's restaurant, I took Aziz with me to have tea and he began opening up to me. He told me how he had always wanted to become a qawwal, right from the time when the great Ismail Azad had taken him under his esteemed wings. Aziz had a very clear and loud voice and like all singers he was the secondary singer to Ismail Azad.

After a couple of years Aziz ventured out on his own and only had three musicians to accompany him, playing the harmonium, tabla and banjo. Aziz's style was unique compared to other well-known qawwals, at the time. After the date of our qawwali night was set, my friends and I made all the arrangements in the compound including serving tea or coffee after about two hours when the singer took a break. Ordinarily, qawaalis started ten in the evening and continued to five in the morning. The program was an absolute hit, with all the guests congratulating Aziz for his performance and me and my friends for arranging the qawaali. Aziz was pleased with all the arrangements and thus was the beginning of life-long friendship, whereby we became brothers.

Rajab's house was right behind Gulshan Nani's house and was next to Qassam's the librarian. Next to them lived Gulandoon with her two sons. Ibrahim and Abdullah. Gulandon's forefathers had come to Iran from Africa and later migrated to

Bombay. Her family was one of the poorest in the compound and she did all the menial work when could get to keep the pot boiling.

Gulandoon did groceries for many in the compound and she would even help me delivering letters to my girlfriends. My mother who loved her a lot helped her as many in the compound. She was also very entertaining so, ladies called her to their homes, and she would make them laugh by telling them jokes laden with foul language which the ladies had never used in their lives and thus enjoyed coming from her.

Gulandoon and my mother loved and confided in each other. My father would often excuse himself as soon as Gulandoon arrived as he was quite shy and definitely not accustomed to the coarse language used. I loved her very much and also helped her a little. She always carried letters to and fro from my girlfriends Rezwan (Pussy Aunty's daughter) and Nosrat (Najafi Aunty's daughter).

Gulandoon's husband, Machin was assigned to a steam ship as a deck hand but was unfortunately an alcoholic. He was also a comedian so after his chores were completed the shipmates and officers would invite him to partake of some booze and entertain them. My uncle, Ali Khan before he became a thoroughbred horse trainer, was a third engineer on the same steam ship. My uncle noticed that Machin was absolutely sloshed every night and it became puzzling because the shipmates were aware that he was only given at most a couple of drinks. Machin being from our compound my uncle looked after him.

One night when everyone else had retired, my uncle followed Machin. What he discovered shocked and flabbergasted him. Machin was caught drinking spirits which in the '30s was used for gas lamps! My uncle pulled him aside and tried to explain to him the serious health consequences.

Machin pleaded with my uncle not to tell the skipper. Sadly, the poor chap eventually succumbed to this bad habit because after he returned onshore and home, he continued to drink he eventually died.

Gulandoon had one brother, Iqbal who met with the same fate as her husband. Her older son Ebrahim sadly was also an alcoholic. He, however, was a stylish guy and despite riddled with empty pockets most of the time, he looked dapper in a suit and hat. Everyone was both bedazzled and befuddled at this guy and could not comprehend from where he got the money to dress so elegantly.

In those days, I used to look after my father's cold drink house during the summer school holidays. Ebrahim used to come in a Victoria carriage to me and say "boss I need some money" it used to make me laugh, here he is booted and suited and a carriage and has no money, a real hustler. I always helped him and one fine day I heard he had died at a prematurely young age.

Gulandoon's younger son Abdullah is a miracle child. He was born premature, his whole body the size of a large palm, his head the size of an apple, he was a wonderful sight to behold, so reminisced my mum for she had seen him at birth. He was born around 1932, six years before I was born when no lifesaving incubators existed. But God had other plans.

His resilient mother kept him in a shoe box filled with cotton and fed him by soaking clean cotton cloth in milk and squeezing the milk into his tiny mouth. Abdullah began gradually gaining strength and weight and finally emerged from the box and was placed with baby clothes. One fine day, Gulandoon came running to my mum, breathless and kept on only repeating "Abdullah Abdullah". My mum feared the six-year-old Abdullah had passed away. My mum beseechingly yelled at her to tell her what had happened to Abdullah. With a wide smile, while catching her breath exclaimed that Abdullah had learnt to sit and broke a cup of milk.

Everybody in the house smiled with relief and knew Abdullah was here to stay!

I was then only one year old, and Abdullah and I grew up to be the best of friends during an era when no one saw the colour of one's skin or how rich or poor one was. We became best friends and by the grace of God he is still alive. The only bad habit Abdullah has which he acquired in later life is smoking opium. He walked daily at least four times, to and fro from the mosque for prayers, which was four miles away. In that way he was very religious and everybody loved him.

The school I attended was St. Mary High School and was located right next to Aga Hall and separated by walls, so was just less than ten minutes' walk from my house. I was six years old when my sister Bibi Tela enrolled, me to the school, the first two years were known as junior and secondary, and it then took another eight years to matriculate. Now a days one requires nine more years to graduate from high school which is presently known as Secondary School Certificate (SSC).

One day while the class teacher was teaching another teacher excused herself for interrupting and asked the boys who were in the school play to come for rehearsals after class. I innocently asked why I was not asked about my interest in taking part in the play. From the age of five I was good at mimicry and everyone loved me for making them laugh. Luckily, all the parts were not taken, and I got a role singing and tap dancing.

It was the 1940s and India was still under the British colonial rule. Most Indians, who had attended English schools had learned dancing and singing from this western influence, especially American songs tap dancing, fox trot and jiving. We had no coach, but we all learnt from watching Hollywood movies. The day before the play I developed a bout of real big jitters and kept on rehearsing the song and dance in our house. It was an American song from the South with lyrics "I've come from Alabama with the banjo on my knees I'm going to Louisiana for my true love to see.." which I kept on singing while practicing the tap-dancing.

Finally, seven children were fully rehearsed and ready to perform on stage. Behind the curtains we changed costumes with our face and hands painted black with water colour paint fashioned as Negro minstrels with each of us given a slice of watermelon to hold.

From behind the curtains we could hear the voices of friends and family who were eagerly waiting for the curtains to rise. Our nervousness accelerated as the curtains went up and the clapping and cheering filled the auditorium. We sauntered to the center of the stage and all our nervousness disappeared.

The show was a big hit with parents clapping and cheering endlessly during a standing ovation. The performing child actors bowed with great joy and pride; we were undoubtedly the little heroes of the day. Endless hugs by parents, friends and teachers congratulating us all a great moment, I can never forget.

I was bitten by the acting bug and during the next two years I was cast in lead roles. With this experience and resume I wanted to venture out and try my luck in the Indian film Industry. My little brain began thinking who could get me access to the film studios. Months went by and I kept asking everybody I knew, if they or any of their friends had any connections to the film studios. All they had to do was just get me in and leave the rest to me. After all I was my father's son, who had the confidence to do something deemed practically impossible. I had the same chutzpah and confidence, so I was persistent in my endeavour and as luck would have it, I met a Punjabi Muslim fellow who was a camera trolley boy in the studios.

The Aga Khan compound also had a very narrow back entrance next to my Granny's house. A Punjabi chap used to always pass by and wish salaams to my granny. I asked myself why not ask him if he could take me to the studios. So, one day I mustered up courage and childishly asked him. In his calm and relaxed manner, he agreed. To me that "yes" was the sweetest I had heard.

However, after agreeing he asked why I wanted to visit. Was I interested in watching the shooting of movies. I told him it was my dream to act in any child star roles in the movies.

He promised me that he would take me in but 1 had to remember that after all he was just a trolley boy. The day arrived to actually visit the studios, I was told to be dressed up and ready to leave by five am. I was ready by four and sitting on the steps of Granny's house waiting. Finally, the Punjabi boy - I don't even remember his name - arrived at five am. We walked to the main gate and boarded the double-decker which stopped right opposite the big gate of the compound. We arrived at the studio's gate and lie took permission from the gate watchman to allow me in. I was dressed up in short pants, a shirt and my school tie. As we entered the film studios, my first ever step into such a glamourous domain, I could hear my heart thumping so loudly that I imagined it would jump out of my chest.

I was in the film studios! My new friend pointed out the director whose name was Jagdish Sethi, well known in those days for both directing and acting. All of a sudden I courageously and gingerly walked up to him between takes and said, "Namaste Mr. Sethi I want to act in the movies. He was busy discussing something with the producer. He looked at me and smiled and directed me to sit next to him while he finished his discussions. I would be lying if I told you I was not scared, but I was determined to go through with it. He finally turned to me and asked me why I wanted to act in the movies. For money? I quickly said no and did not hesitate and told him I loved to act and about my experience on the stage.

Jagdish Sethi was impressed by my courage, enthusiasm and ambition and while talking to me he had a kind, fatherly and encouraging smile. He asked his assistant to give me instructions and after a few moments he returned and handed me an address. The assistant told me that I should meet another of the director's assistant who would instruct me further.

I could not believe I was on the way to becoming an actor. In my giddying excitement I must have thanked Jagdish Sethi a thousand times He embraced me and told me to go and have a screen test he had arranged, and he would take it from there. The address was Famous Studios in Mahalaxmi, which I believe still exists today and where most top producers and directors had their offices.

Mahalaxmi was about four miles from my house. I would wake up every morning at six and go jogging with my close friend Charlie, brother of my first true love Nosrat. We went out jogging but being completely pooped returned walking. We were very much ahead of our times as this was 1940s when jogging was not heard of. People would watch us wondering whom these kids are running from.

So boarding the bus to go to the Studios I continued to pray till I reached because I was about to give a screen test about which I had no idea. When I arrived, I showed the note to the receptionists and she directed me to the first floor room. The peon directed me to sit in the office where right in front of me was a life-size photo of the great and beautiful actress Naseem Banu. Later I came to know that she was the mother of another great beautiful actress Saira Banu, wife of the legend Dilip Kumar.

After about fifteen minutes, which felt like hours filled with anxiety not knowing what I was expected to do, a pleasant guy came and called out my name Alladin. I jumped up and he told me to follow him. He took rue down to a room where a large camera was nestled on its tripod. He instructed me to be myself and follow the guiding instructions of the cameraman who would take three or four head shots. I did not know what 'head shots' meant but I assumed it meant my close-up photos.

After I was through with the head shots, I was sent to another room which appeared to be soundproof where I gave my sound test. I was given about ten lines which the assistant sound engineer told me take a few minutes to memorize. After a few takes I was finished with the tests at which point the assistant director told me that Jagdishji would contact me.

It was more than a week that I had not heard from Jagdish Sethi and I was slowly giving up hope, but finally a messenger came with a letter from the director. In the letter Jagdish Sethi congratulated me and informed me in detail about my role. I was to play the younger version of the hero Shyam in the film Shabistan and it was quite a big role. I ran to my mother who supported me and encouraged me from the very start with the good news and she was elated with a big smile of joy spreading on her face.

She only now hoped that my father would agree. She said she would speak to him extremely tactfully at an opportune moment. My dad, a hard worker came home around midnight after shutting the restaurant and sat with my mum who served him dinner. He used to take one or two pegs of country booze and soda and then take his dinner. As soon as he had finished his drink, my mum told him that she had good news about me.

All eight children were fast asleep at that time except me. I was anxiously waiting to see and hear my father's reaction. As soon as my mother told him that I was to act in the film he angrily yelled that he would break my legs if I stepped into the studios. I felt like a ton of bricks had fallen on me and I sobbed for a long time, muttering to myself that one day I would still became an actor, how I did not know.

More seriously, we heard the sad news that Shyam had died on the spot when he had fallen off his horse while shooting a scene in the film, I had wished to make my acting debut. What is puzzling actually director Bihbuti Mitra directed Shabistan, but I distinctly remember I spoke with director Jagdish Sethi, maybe I met him when he was directing Do Dil. Although I had lost my chance to act in films, I did not lose hope to get another chance to fulfil my dreams. Meanwhile I had the school plays where I always landed the lead role.

Like all schools, we had a class prefect who was a mean bully and larger than the rest of us. As I was popular in class, he made it a point to pick on me habitually. As the class waited for the teacher to arrive, the bullying prefect would take the board dusted and hit on the back of my head with the wooden side with me crying out in pain each time. Actually, all the students were scared of him and did not want to get on his wrong side.

The bullying continued until one fine day I decided that I must do something about it, enough is enough. The bell for the morning recess rang. All the children ran to play on the school grounds. I found the bully standing with some of his friends. I mustered all my courage and gingerly walked up to him and before he could say anything, I caught him by surprise and pushed him as hard as I could!

He fell to the ground and I jumped on him, caught both his ears and started pounding his head on the ground. As I was beating the life out of him, I kept on repeating "take-take-take," meaning take a taste of your own medicine.

If my friends would not have grabbed and dragged me away, I don't know what would have happened to him. The back of his head was noticeably swollen. We were summoned to the office of the principal, Father Molina, a Jesuit priest from Spain who was a very kind soft-spoken man. He questioned me about my unusual atypical behaviour. After I told him my reasons, he dismissed us by scolding the bully. From then on the bully respected me.

In school we had one recess at eleven in the morning for fifteen minutes. Lunch was at one p.m. for an hour with another recess at 3 p.m. We made the best of this free time, and played games mostly robbers and thieves, I don't know why we called it robbers and thieves because essentially, they both meant the same thing. One team played the role of the police and the other thieves. The game was different from hide - and - seek which came after it.

If team police spotted a thief, they ran towards them to catch them. One day I was being chased by the police playmate, tripped, fell and landed my head on the raised section of the cement seating around the tree. The sound was so loud I thought I had cracked my skull. Blood started gushing out with my friends rushing me home while holding a handkerchief and pressing on the wound on my forehead.

Luckily, my hero, my sister Bibi Tela had come from her school, and she rushed me to Dr. Telang who had his clinic behind our house in Love Lane. He applied a yellow ointment and bandaged my forehead. Bibi took me to the doctor to change the dressing for a few days and soon I was good as new.

When you are young your injuries heal quicker. I still bear the scar and when I am shaving and looking in the mirror my eyes always go straight to the scar which immediately reminds me the sweet pain of my wonderful school days. Our school principal always told us those days would be the best days of our lives and they would never come back, and we would miss them. Very true.

During the monsoons, although we were walking distance from the house, we were not allowed to go home for lunch. The parents of all students gave lunch money to their kids. Near the school there was an Iranian restaurant about twenty steps away from the school gates. Even if it rained cats and dogs, for days, we would do a hundred meter' sprint to the restaurant and buy hot boroon kheema - Hindi for' round crusty bread with minced meat in it like a sandwich. Boy how I miss it.

All the vendors were available, come rain or shine, they would come to our compound. One of them was an Arab who had settled in Bombay. He used to ride a large three wheeled cycle. On the front two wheels was attached a big insulated box filled with hot small kababs, samosas and other delicacies. He used to call out in a loud voice to draw peoples' attention. In his strong Arab accent, he would shout "garama -garam" (have them hot), paying a big emphasis on the mutton balls. We used to laugh and run out to buy the tasty treats. To date my friends remember him.

Bhaiyyas, who came from Uttar Pradesh side of India, sold bhel puris a savoury snack. It is made of puffed rice, vegetables and a tangy tamarind sauce, and has a crunchy texture. They always came with a delicious aroma and were another great snack. Oh yes, there was also Kaka (meaning uncle) who carried a heavy bag on his shoulder which seemed to have everything you could imagine, from small hot onion samosas to used postal stamps from all countries (those days kids collected stamps).

Summer holidays were from April to May right after our final exams. We would wait anxiously for the results which came by mail to our house. The report paper was on good quality paper. If you failed any subject a red line appeared below the subject. If you failed in four subjects you had to repeat the class. Within a week after the exams the results arrived. With my heart thumping I used to open the mail and always held onto the reverse side to see if any red lines were visible. There were thankfully no red lines. I had passed and let go a sigh of relief.

During the summer holidays my father always made me, to my dismay, go to our cold drink house to work. I had to wake up at five a.m. in the morning, travel by bus and then walk about four miles an open the shop. I worked there for a week. Then I was allowed to go home refresh and come back. In the day my father sat as a cashier, twelve noon he went home and had his lunch, napped for an hour, wake up had tea and returned to the cold drink house.

Summer was the busiest season as people used to come to the cold drink house to get relief from the weather, the most popular and their favourite drink was soda lemon mix., and other different sodas. The waiter took the orders, brought the soda and lemon to me. I used to pop the bottles, opening with dexterity, holding three bottles in each hand between the fingers and pouring while mixing the soda and lemon. Of course, there were other soft drinks including the sherbats.

By noon, only few people came, and my dad went home. I changed into my dry clothes as I was drenched with the water splashed on rue, while I had washed the glasses. By three p.m. my father was back, and I continued the same routine till nine p.m. It was more or less one or two customers till eleven p.m. Our restaurant was right opposite a Marathi cinema house. Eleven p.in. was time for the movie interval and then we had the last rush of the day. Then my father counted all the money and took it home with him.

We employed two waiters. Pandiya and Dhatoo and "a manager" by name only he was older than the other two who were barely sixteen years old. All went home with the exception of Dhatoo. We closed shop and he mopped the whole shop clean and spotless. We used to rent two cycles and, in the night, went to Chowpaty Beach which was open all night. You could get anything you wanted to eat there, and we ate our dinner which was served on banana leaves.

For dessert, we used to eat Kulfi (Indian ice cream). We walked with our cycles away from the crowd and slept on the sand with one arm on our cycles lest someone would rob us. We were up at dawn, cycling back to the shop to resume the routine.

Already at the age of ten, I had an unrivalled talent for loving girls. I had three things going for me: I was bold, was an incorrigible flirt and had the gift of the gab. I put all my talents to use and managed to hook four girls at the same time. They all knew each other as they all played in the compound. They each believed and presented that they were the only ones for me as I had deceptively assured them that it was so.

The names of the girls were Guboo who was our neighbour and lived two houses from us. Very cute, her complexion was like coffee mixed with condensed milk. Then there was Fato, whose house was attached to Guboo's. She was dark with a pretty face with a good figure. I admit I was bad as I used these girls to pass time.

The other two girls were Rezwan, Pussy aunty's daughter and Nosrat, Najafi aunty's youngest daughter. They were closer to my heart than Guboo and Fato. Nosrat was, in fact, my very first true love and will remain in my heart till I die. Rezwan and Nosrat were cousins and all of us were closely attached. Pussy aunty knew about my liking for Rezwan and she kind of liked me. Our family was the only one which was allowed to visit her house, from all of the compound.

Najafi aunty tried her best to keep Nosrat and me apart, hence I was not welcome nor allowed to visit her house although Ezzat and Charly, Nosrat's sister and brother, were close friends of mine. Ezzat was a real sister to me and she loved and was in favour of me. She was about six years older than I same age as my sister Bibi Tela. She always told us that her mother had big plans for Nosrat.

Ezzat was the darling of all the young people in the compound but not their parents. But she did not give a tuppence about all their ill words and gossips about her demeanour and behaviour. The elders felt like she was too brazen, but all the youngsters loved her and wished they could be like her, especially the girls. One must remember that the late 1940s was an era when everybody was kind of reserved and stiff upper-lipped. They held old fashioned values and Ezzat enraged them by doing what she wanted to do.

She had many male platonic friends, but the gossip brigade used to have a field day with her. Ezzat used to flaunt her friendships in front of them, though she was not promiscuous or anything but loved to tease the hell out of these elders who enjoyed gossiping vociferously about her.

Ezzat was best friends with my sisters and she loved and would help me with Nosrat. By this time, we were in our teens and I spent more of my time with Nosrat. One day Ezzazt got me eight cinema tickets to an Indian film 'Amber' starring the famous couple Raj Kapoor and Nargis.

But how to sneak Nosrat out of the house, so she could join me and my other friends? I went to Rubab aunty, a widow, who had live children. She had a great respect for my mother. Boys often gathered at her house for tea and snacks. She loved us all as we loved her. Rubab Aunty and all others in the compound, knew about my love for Nosrat. I pleaded with her to get permission from Nosrat's mum. She was to tell her that all the girls were going to the cinema and she would be the chaperon. Najafi Aunty agreed and gave permission for Nosrat to go!

The gang of eight was chaperoned by Rubab aunty and included my sister Meher; Rezwan; two of Rubab aunty's daughters; Guboo; Nosrat; and one more I don't remember, and myself, the only male member of the entourage. I gave the six tickets to Aunty and exchanged mine and Nosrat's ticket to go sit in the box seats, paying the difference for the upgrade.

Each box had only two seats for love birds, Nosrat and I occupied the box which was right above the others were seated. Rezwan was sitting next to my sister and was raging with jealousy. She continued to ask my sister, why I was treating her this way. It was my fault that I did not inform Aunty not to invite Rezwan. I really felt for her and I knew how to wake up with her, and I later did. But the poor thing went through an agonizing three hours!

My mother was very much in favour of Nosrat. She always said that she would love her to be her daughter-in-law. I usually arranged the compound picnics with boys and girls all together, arranging the bus transport through my school friend Torab whose father worked with private bus companies.

Next to our compound there was an ice factory. We used to buy a big slab of ice covered with sawdust to prevent it from melting; sherbats from my dad's cold drink house and biryani (spicy rice and mutton dish) which my mum made while the others brought snacks. This was one of the best and most memorable moments of our lives.

My eldest sister Firouze went to Nosrat's house asking permission to have Nosrat join us at the picnic. As anticipated Nosrat's mum kindly refused my sister. Ezzat convinced her mum, since she was going and Nosrat would be fine with her, with a little more persuasion she agreed. When I heard I was overcome with a sigh of relief and joy.

At six in the morning, the bus was loaded with food, snacks, sherbat drinks, and finally the girls and boys embarked the bus. We began the trip to Juhu Beach and just before leaving we picked up the ice from the ice factory outside the compound. Juhu Beach was about twelve miles away and we reached there by seven thirty.

Picnic mats were laid out on the sand under the coconut trees. We all sat down for our morning tea. All of us had brought our flasks and with the hot tea we had samosas for breakfast. With our bellies full we started playing Tennikoit for a couple of hours, rested then went swimming.

Nosrat and I walked about four hundred yards away from everyone for our privacy. We splashed in the water for a long time till lunch time. My mum had laid out a long mat for all of us to sit around. She asked Nosrat to sit next to her for she loved her very much, and I sat next to her.

Earlier while swimming I had asked Nosrat about her mother's plans to take her to Karachi to marry her off to a rich guy. Being really innocent, she did not know anything about it. I then asked Ieer to swear by the ebb of the tide, that we would get married to one another. We took the oath holding hands. We were really in love. As I write and reminisce today, I can still feel the emotions and current which energized us while taking the oath. When Najafi aunty realized she could not keep us apart she sent Nosrat to Bandra to stay with her relatives, a ten-mile bus ride.

Once in a while Nosrat came to the compound, and Rezwan would fume with anger for she knew I would spend more time with Nosrat than her. Rezwan would write a spiteful note informing me the python from Bandra was here and she hoped I would not be seeing her. Nosrat was quite the opposite of a python, she was an angel. My love story had a very sad and heart—breaking ending which I will elaborate in Volume Two.

Meanwhile my uncle Ali Khan was enjoying great success in horse-racing. He raced in Bombay and Poona but most of his racing was Bangalore, Mysore and in the south. He had his own rickshaw with a driver. He had a great loyal, loving man named Hamid who was kind of a real butler who wore many hats, including that of a cook.

On racing days, which were only held on weekends Hamid helped my uncle in the stables. When my uncle's horse won, he would lead the winner along with my uncle.

Our school summer holidays were beginning soon. My uncle had arranged for our family to spend the holidays with him in Bangalore, and reserved the whole train compartment for our family which included seven children, Granny, Mum and Zara Khaleh, wife of Moosa Khan who was also into racing. Zareh Khalela was a real sister to my Mum and we loved her very much. She had two sons, Muhammad Hussein and Essa who was a very handsome man -a bodybuilder and like an elder brother to me.

My father made a big fuss about my going, as usual he wanted me to work at the cold drink house. Luckily, my uncle arrived in Bombay before the summer holidays and he convinced my father that it was fine for me to take a summer break from working non-stop at the shop. My father could never refuse my uncle and I was so excited to finally be embarking on my first extended holiday ever!

It took us one and a half days to reach Bangalore. My uncle and Hamid were waiting at the station for us and the coolies carried our luggage to the taxi. We arrived at the bungalow and were immediately in awe that we were going to live in such a big house for two months for the first time.

Hamid made sure all the food was prepared. He was a great cook and he took care of all the children as if we were his own. In the afternoon he took us to a Hindu restaurant where we all had masala dosa-an Indian specialty made of spicy mashed potatoes rolled into a quite long dough that was then deep fried. Oh my God, this was a snack to die for, paired with South Indian coffee and end-noted with a sweet pan and we were in gastronomic heaven! This was our routine snack each afternoon and we desired nothing else.

Sometimes Hamid would take me to my uncle's stables; I enjoyed being with the racehorses in their private stalls where I would pet them. From that moment, my love for horses was deeply embedded in my heart and when I was around thirty-five years old. I learned to ride with an English girl as my instructor. I will elaborate in Volume Three.

We were living the best times of our lives which was suddenly all jinxed. All of a sudden from out of nowhere, one morning we woke up to find that both our hands were covered with large boils covering the whole of our palms. Five of us experienced this malady excepting our two elder sisters. Firouze nursed us, pressing the boils from the sides to get all the pus out, washing the areas thoroughly with Dettol, applying ointment and bandaging both wands. Twice a day she lovingly took care of us and as suddenly as they had come the boils disappeared in about five days.

Zahrals Khaleh and my Mum pampered us during this ordeal as did my granny which helped in easing the pain which, did not, however, stop us from going for our afternoon snacks with Hamid. Since our hands were bandaged, we could not eat or drink. Hamid took car e of that and lovingly fed all of us and did not make us feel helpless. We will never forget this wonderful man, who was in our lives for only two months but who we still talk about decades later.

My uncle asked us to extend our stay because he wanted to take us to Mysore and Ooty. My older sister Bibi Tela and I were concerned about our studies, and thus returned home although I was already late a week for school. The following day when I went to school, I went to join try friends in the class and tried to catch up on what I load missed. The teacher began the roll call and when I did not hear my name I went and asked her why I had been left out. She told me to go to the principal's office for an explanation.

Our dear father Molina had been replaced by a new principal, Father Brito who informed me that I had been dismissed from school for arriving a week late. I was shocked and could not believe what I was hearing, and tears began to well in my eyes. In a soft voice I questioned the new principal about the harsh punishment for being just one week late. He was a man of the cloth, someone who is supposed to be kind and compassionate, and not be so harsh with a mere child. Instead of kindness in a gruff, loud and mean tone he informed we bluntly that he had no time to explain and that I should pick up my books and go home.

My sister Bibi Tela accompanied me to school the next day to plead with this idiotically stubborn Father. She asked him to hear her out with which he replied harshly to keep it brief. She imploringly explained to him that we lived just next door and that I had attended this school from my childhood.

Despite the explanation he was again rude and said that it was not possible for me to attend this school anymore. All the students hated him as much as we all loved Father Molina. So that was the end of my school days at St. Mary School.

As far as my further education was concerned, my sister Bibi Tela took care of it. She decided that the best alternative to St. Mary, was St. Isabel School. My older sister Meher and my younger brother Saifudin were already attending that school. The principal of St. Isabel was Daisy Baptista, who was also a very strict disciplinarian. A few of the compound kids also attended this school. Without any further ado, my sister got me enrolled.

By this time, I had missed three weeks of school, and the new curriculum was much harder here. Normally it takes a long time to make new friends, but three students became friends with me on the very first day. They were Noordin known as Nokoo, Vijay and Qassam. Nokoo was my sister

Meher's boyfriend. They were really very much in love, like a modern-day Romeo and Juliette. It was a co-educational school, and there were plenty of girls, so I was as happy as a tom cat in a milking barn!

The lessons were inordinately difficult, and it took a lot of hard work to get used to the new curriculum. The school was founded by the Baptists, and it was now run by three spinster sisters, Daisy, Lilly and Violette. Daisy was the principal; Lilly took care of all the administration work with Violette helping her. A fourth sister was married to Mr. Miranda and her son was in my class.

The Baptists were devout Catholics and Daisy and her sisters went to church early in the morning to the church - which was opposite our compound, lodged right inside the grounds of St Mary School Cambridge section - from where they went straight to school.

St. Isabel School is located at the same address since 1885 and celebrated its 1 25th anniversary a decade ago. The Baptists lived in a large house opposite to the school perched on a hill. They started a small school from this house till they worked their way to what it is today, one of the most prestigious high school in Bombay. It is by no means a heritage structure but remains proudly part of the local history.

Back to my school days. I continued to act in school plays and most of the time, Nokoo and I landed leading roles. Being the ardent playboy, I continued to flirt with girls and had plenty to choose from. I am not speaking out of self- adulation but my second year I had five girlfriends, Joginder, Shamsi, Mabel, Audrey and Erusha who was senior to us.

I had five but there was a Sikh girl Nirmala, who lived in the building opposite the school. She had a very sweet face but was proud and reserved and hardly ever smiled. I vowed to myself that I must procure her as my girlfriend. So, I began using all my charming wiles on her but to no avail. My expertise on girls kept on reassuring me that she was interested, but too proud to admit and let alone show it.

As mentioned earlier, we used to play Tennikoit, a game played on a tennis- type court with a circular, hard rubber ring hurled over the net separating the players; each endeavouring to catch and return it to the opposite court.

One lucky day (I will explain later why lucky), one of the players from the opposite team hurled the ring instead of returning to our side of the court. It flew over the wall to the neighbour's. To keep thieves and intruders from breaking in from either side, the top of the wall was covered with shards of broken sharp glass embedded on top of concrete.

No kid dared to jump over the wall to fetch the Tennikoit. I noticed Nirmala watching us playing and her eyes were glued onto me. I decided to jump over the wall. I needed at least 10 to 1 2 feet to gain moment to run and go over the high wall. I jumped, held my arm as high as possible while simultaneously making a big arch with my arm. This would avoid my arm getting ripped by the sharp— edged glass. I made it over successfully and the crowd of school nates started cheering, I found the rubber ring and tossed it over on to our side with which came more cheering.

Now l had to recreate the same manoeuvre to return to the school side. Again I needed to run before I jumped, unfortunately I only load only about three feet of space. I ran towards the wall and jumped as high as l could. But it was not enough, I could not make it. With all my strength, 1 jumped again. This time around I held onto the edge on our side and felt the palm of my had straining and again more cheering. Unfortunately, my hand slipped and the arch of my arm was not enough to keep the sharp edges of the glass away from my arm. The sharp splinters ripped deep into the flesh of my under arm close to my armpit. I held on and climbed to our side of the wall.

Suddenly all cheering stopped when they saw my arm bleeding profusely. Nirmala repeatedly pretended that she was not interest in me but she was the first to come and tell me off asking why I always had to be the hero. She had the presence of mind to take me to the doctor whose clinic was just outside our school, accompanied by friends Nokoo and Vijay. Upon checking my arm, the doctor informed the gash was one inch deep and about two inches long.

Mostly in such cases doctors put stitches, but this doctor, after disinfecting the wound only applied a thick layer of yellow calming ointment. Bandaging me, he told me to come daily to change the dressing. In the eyes of the kids I was a hero, but more importantly I got Nirmala. I still have the scar.

In school all my girlfriends were close to my sister but the closest was Joginder and Shamsi who came to our house regularly. I was no more a kid and was beyond puppy love. I was in my teens so had become a little aggressive in pursuing and romancing girls. In our house I took the girls behind the curtains and kissed and necked.

But I never took advantage of the situation with any of the girls I was with even though a couple of them pleaded with me to go all the way. I always pushed them away at the right time. In that way I was very honourable. I respected the girls and always believed they should save themselves for their wedding night.

We finally got to our last year of high school. Our class teacher was Daisy and she was both a principal, and French teacher. The whole school was scared of her. The first thing in the morning when we were seated in our respected classes, Ms. Daisy would start her rounds from one end of the corridor to the other end.

Even though each class had its own respective teacher, if she caught any student talking when the teachers' back was turned, she would chastise the student in a loud voice. Her voice was so loud that students out of fear sat straight in all classes across the corridor. But not Nokoo, Vijay and myself.

We actually challenged her in many ways.

The Baptists, especially Lilly loved the charity work. From the age of six I was taught by my granny to think of those who were less fortunate. We were given only one anna pocket money when going to school.

In those days sixteen annas made a Rupee. If one were to convert it to Dollars, it would be about less than 10 cents.

During the school recess we often bought roasted chickpeas or peanuts for five cents we would get a cone shaped paper full of the nuts. I used to share with my classmates, some of whom were poor. This made me feel good. By the grace of God, from that age to now I continue my charity work as much as I can.

I have inculcated this charitable habit in my children, and grandchildren, and I pray they do the same for their offsprings. We must have been taught by God in our sacred book, the Holy Quran to share from the sustenance God has given us, to the less fortunate a minimum of two and half percent from our earnings. First your deserving kin, then orphans, then the needy. If the whole world followed this principal, then one would never see any poverty in the world.

Unfortunately, the filthy rich, in their greed, steal from the poor in so many ways, which we all know, instead of sharing part of their income. After school activities, we had drama classes and plays. Every year parents, and (friends came to watch the annual school play. Unlike St Mary School, at the new school parents paid an entrance fee to watch their children perform.

The money collected went in a kitty for the lepers in Surat, Gujrat.

We also held annual funfair that included games like knocking down stacked wooden bottles; shooting at small balloons, among other fun activities including snacks, cakes and sweetmeats all of which brought in good money and all for the charity, which parents knew about and hence they spent freely.

All the money collected helped us buy cookies dried fruits and canned food. Used and new clothes donated by parents also helped the needy a great deal. Thankfully, it used to be quite a load of charity bestowed.

All the boys and girls who made this possible, were chosen to go to Surat and personally deliver the goods to the lepers.

The leper community was run by nuns and sisters, supervised by a father. Most of the clergy was either from Spain or Ireland and each of them had dedicated their lives to help the leper home. In those days it took longer than nowadays to travel this distance to Surat. Upon arrival the nuns greeted us, and one room was already prepared for all of us. The nuns and father were truly elated to see us. After unrolling our mattresses beds-for this was no luxury hotel - the nuns fed us with boiled vegetables and potatoes. We first slurped the soup and after that we ate the vegetables and potatoes.

We collected money for food and clothing for the lepers every year. On one of these trips I contracted conjunctivitis in both eyes. When we arrived at the leper home, one of the sisters saw my eyes and comforted me. After washing my eyes, she applied some ointment, which was soothing. She was very young and pretty and while her head and mouth were very close to me, the naughty boy that I was, I was on the verge of kissing her on her lips!

We usually stayed there for three or four days. We were always taken around the leper home and saw the poor disfigured face of men women and children. They looked so helpless, yet when they saw us approaching, to show their appreciation they bowed their heads and touched their fingerless hands to their foreheads.

It was visually very disturbing to see humans suffer from a disease for which there was no cure. This gave us a lot of clarity and encouragement to work even harder for them. The father and nuns were trained nurses and one had to take ones' hats off to them. We always prayed for them, as one day we received the sad news one of the nuns had contracted the disease but continued serving the lepers. That level of dedication still leaves me speechless.

The leper home in Surat still exists, but now it's a much larger compound with modern medicine and equipment compared to the time we were there in the 1950s.

It was table-tennis tournament day. Students from fifth grade to eleventh grade were eligible to participate. When the games began those, who lost were eliminated. I qualified at each round and was a favourite to win. Every time I played, my girlfriends were there to applaud me and eventually I qualified for the finals.

The day arrived for the finals and the whole school was there to watch. My opponent was a short boy who was quite well built and was a great player. His name was Saeed and he lived in the Padamsee Wadi which belonged to Nokoo's dad and uncle.

Nokoo, Vijay, Qassam and all my girlfriends were there to cheer and support me. Every time I smashed a difficult shot the girls shouted at the top of their lungs. I was so engrossed in pleasing my girlfriends, that I started showing off risking the most difficult shots, which cost me the championship. If I had not started showing off to the girls I would have won.

I was also becoming the foremost actor of the school. Right behind was Nokoo and Mickey, a catholic boy who was always cast in the role of a comedian. Ms. Daisy, our principal, now put rue in charge of producing and directing plays of the whole school. By the grace of God, I proved my mettle, and always put up a great show.

After I left school, Peter Miranda my class irate, a nephew of Ms. Daisy, became the principal. Being my classmate, we graduated together, and he remained a close friend. A few years after my school days, I received a letter from Peter. In my honour he had initiated a best actor cup known as Alladin's Cup.

It was presented every year to the best actor of the school who got to keep it for a year. Next year it was passed on to the best actor of that year. Peter left so did the tradition of handing out that cup. I believe Peter died young.

Vijay and I were the smartest in the class. Our interest were the same and we decided we would become medical doctors. Even after sixty years 1 can still recount a human's whole anatomy. Vijays's house was on the fourth floor of a building opposite to the backside of my Granny's house. We connected with each other by whistling the famous American tune "Cherry Pink and Apple Blossom White".

I totally forgot to mention that Hadi Jalali was also a very good friend. He attended school with us at St Isabel. He lived in Love Lane, in a big compound. Hadi lived on the top floor with his large family of eight children: Sadiq, Hashim, Marzieh,

Siddiqueh, Assad, Hadi, Khatu and Abbas. The mother Abaji, was a very close friend of my mum's. At least twice a week, she just walked across Love Lane and would enter our compound. The two friends had tea, snacks, and gossiped while smoking cigarette. Sometimes Abaji related tales of the scary occurrences in their house which was really haunted.

Baqer was a very strong man; tall and tough as they get, and our Iranian community was proud of him. He could bend a horseshoe in one hand, and he was not scared of ghostly spirits. Their (family's house had a large verandah where Baqer slept. The daily newspaper was laid out on a table, close to Baqer's bed. In the still of midnight, with no existing breeze, a spirit would seep through the newspaper, rustling it and aggravating Baqer enough to wake him up.

Baqer was used to the nuisance of the apparition and nothing could scare him. While addressing the spirit, he would shout "Get lost you bastard, you don't scare me!" The spirit would leave him and go to try and scare the others. It had the whole night to scare everyone.

The house-servant, a woman in her sixties used to sleep on the floor next to Abaji's bed. Sometimes, the spirit used to slowly drag her and place her right next to the toilet! One-night Abaji woke up to drink water, she found an invisible hand pouring drinking water in a glass from the jug. This scared the life out of her. On summer nights the windows were kept open to let in the cool breeze. One cool night Siddiqeh saw a scary and ugly monster's face outside of her bedroom window.

Sadiq, the eldest was very strict and all his brothers and sisters respected him. He could get angry if any of his siblings, stepped out of the line. His wife Dulhan a very pretty woman was shy and kind. A Parsi family lived on the ground floor but their abode was free of the spirits which haunted the top floor.

Hadi and I were about the same age. He was a handsome boy with dimples and curly hair. He was very naughty and a great cyclist. At lunch time I rode with him in front of his cycle, double seat to return home. He used to ride really fast, dodging and zigzagging between people walking on the streets. Bhaiiyas usually shaved and oiled their heads. In those days there was hardly any traffic, so these Bhaiiyas used to walk freely on the streets; their oily skulls shining in the sun, being a temptation Hadi could never resist. He would ask me to hold on tight, and I knew what he was about to do. With great skill and speed, our ankles just inches away from the ground, he continued to slap the inviting bald heads. By the time they realized we were gone with the wind.

Hadi and I sometimes played in his compound. One day he dared me to jump from their window to grab a tree branch which was at quite a distance which in hindsight was a bad suggestion. I was not crazy and daring like him. We stood at window ledge and Hadi was about to jump with me pleading with him not to jump. But he jumped and missed the branch by a few inches and fell from the first floor. Both his legs broke, and he was rushed to the hospital. He returned home with both legs plastered. After about five days, this brat was limping precariously and chasing the football.

In our compound Aga Hall, I had a good friend, more like an older brother called Sadru. He was about three years older than me. He was a champion boxer, and led Mahrashtra, in boxing rankings. He taught me to how to box, making me practice rigorously with the punching bags. I became a good boxer but never got an opportunity to enter a boxing ring. My mother was forever worried that I would get seriously injured.

Another friend was Mahinood who we supported in every respect. Later he turned to be the worst kind of human being, which I will expound in Volume Three. But for now, Sadru, Mahmoud and myself were known as 'Three Musketeers.'

All three of us had close friends and relatives in Poona. Sadru's parents actually lived there. Once a month he would travel from Bombay to Poona on his cycle. The journey was around 120 miles by road. The grueling part was from the foot of Khapoli to its peak. It was essentially a vertical uphill ride. If one was cycling the only way was to push the cycle to the top about 15 miles.

For Sadru essentially it was no big deal, or so we thought. Later we came to know how he tackled it. That story will follow. I loved challenges and adventure. I said to myself, "If Sadru can do it, then I could as well." I put the idea to Hadi and he immediately agreed to do it together. the plan included Hadi; Mahmoud from our compound;

Keki a Parsi from our school who would join us on this adventure.

We arranged with cycle shop—owner on Love Lane right behind our house to open the shop at four a.m. in the morning and when we would pick up the bikes.

We could not tell our parents that we were going on this adventure. It would have been impossible for their consent. I told my mum instead that we were going on school picnic to Poona by train.

Mahmoud slept in our house and at three thirty in the morning we awoke and so did my sister Firouze. She packed snacks; egg sandwiches; water bottles, and lastly but not the least tea in thermos. All of us were punctual so at four a.m. we collected our cycles and in the name of God began our adventure.

The only source of light in the darkness, came from the oil lamps which were in the centre of the cycles. We could hardly see but after two hours the most welcome sun rose above the horizon. We did not have to strain our eyes anymore.

We were four hours into the journey. We had left the suburbs behind us, and now we were on a stretch on an asphalt road surrounded by rolling hills leading down to a lush forest filled with Tamarind trees, full of Tamarinds. We looked at one another, and decided we had to stop here, and enjoy the bounties of God.

The tamarinds were generally raw, green and crisp but red inside, and all sweet and sour. We had our fill and collected some for afterwards. Seven hours had passed, and the pedalling was gradually taking its toll. We were getting anxious for we had still not reached Khapoli, the foot of the Western Ghats. But at around 11 a.m., we finally arrived.

Exhausted, we sat in the shade. It was hot and we were sweating profusely. All that was left from our food resources were a few snacks and water. Now the most difficult task of the journey began, pushing our cycle up the vertically inclined Ghats. After every thirty steps we stopped. At this time, we were losing our resolve thinking that this expedition was nothing more than a childish and fantastical idea.

We kept assuring each other that once we reached the top, it would be easy all the way. After a gruelling three and half hours, we reached the top which is called Behramji Point. We had conquered our version of Mount Everest: took in our fill of the scenery from the top, and we were on our way down. There was no more pedalling any more as it was all downwards. We reassured ourselves that within hours we would reach Poona. All the uphill slopes had been climbed, we still had to continue pedalling and by this time we had sores on our backside. To limit the sores from getting worse we stood while cycling. The sun was setting, and Poona was nowhere in sight! About seven miles were left, but we had no idea of the distance. It was now pitch dark, and the oil lamps of the cycles hardly lit the front wheel.

Suddenly, Mahmoud fell to the ground completely exhausted. Hadi asked to stay with Mahmoud and he and Keki would move on. It was fine as Mahmoud was my responsibility. They left and Mahmoud and I were left alone in the darkness. I squinted my eyes and looked around. There were vegetable fields to the right of us and in the distance, I saw a small hut; a glimmer of hope. The hut I assessed was the home of poor farmers.

I helped Mahmoud up and we started walking, pushing our bikes along with us. We arrived at the dilapidated wooden door of the thatched hut whose walls were insulated with cow dung. I knocked at the door twice, and saw a veiled face appear at the window. I knew the Marathi language and respectfully, yet pleadingly said "Aaee" which means mother in Marathi. She leant her head further to assess us and I told her about our sad, and desperate ordeal and situation.

She was convinced we were harmless stranded children and feeling pity for us, she opened the door carrying two large thick quilts with something like a pillow.

Beggars can't be choosers, but everything stank of cow dung which these people were used to. She spread one quilt on a raised square platform around six by six, made of clay and covered with cow dung. And one quilt for protecting us from the cold.

It was a starry night, a sight to behold in awe - the Glory of God. It was so cold we pulled the quilt over our heads. Mahmoud was gone, he started snoring. As if we had less problems, a dog came and made himself comfortable on the quilt next to our feet. I tried to gently push him away, he snarled, and I let him be.

Exhausted physically and mentally, I was drifting off to sleep, when I thought someone calling out my naive distinctly - Alladin —Alladin. As I faded away in deep slumber, so did the voice and so I was sure I was dreaming. I was gone till morning when the kind lady gently called us in the morning to wake us up.

We were sore all over and it pained more than when we were cycling. She had prepared tea and chapati bread. It was the best breakfast of my life, simple but very tasty. She brought some coal embers in a pan to warm our hands and we were very grateful. I gave her five Rupees, worth a lot those days. I learnt from her that Poona was about six miles from her house. Had I known last night I would have tried to convince Mahmoud to muster up courage and continue. Well whatever happens - happens for the best. We began cycling but our backsides were very sore, and the leather seats gave us excruciating pain. We cycled the last half dozen miles standing, until we finally arrived in Poona where our friends welcomed us.

When Hadi arrived Poona last night he told Sadru the approximate place where Mahmoud had given up the journey. The good friend that Sadru was, he set out to help us. He took our friend Jahgan from Poona, and they began calling out my name for a long time. So it was not a dreamt. Sadru and Jhagan came with one cycle double seat. The idea was that if they found us, Jhagan would take Mahmoud on his cycle. These were real friends. As the good old saying goes, "A friend in need is a friend indeed."

We now came to know Sadru's secret. He always hitched a ride on a lorry at the foot of the Ghats; paid a few Rupees to the driver; loaded the cycle on the back of the lorry. From the top of the Ghats he cycled to Poona. If only we knew. Sadru did not know we were planning to cycle or else he would have told us.

On our return to Bombay, we went by train with our cycles in the freight compartment. By now my mother was informed of the ordeal, and on arrival, she immediately gave me a big motherly hug, and then a scolding. Overall, it was a great memorable adventure for kids of fifteen to experience.

After graduation, my dad told me that I should become a lawyer. He tried to soften the blow and reasoned that I was always winning school debates and in elocution I was always scoring a high percentage all of which was true, but my mind was set on becoming a doctor. He even told me that he would send me to England after college to earn my Bar-at-law. But nothing could change my mind.

My father of course had ulterior motives. The first step was to pass the Bachelor's exam, and then off to law school. The B.A. classes was from eight in the morning till eleven. My father wanted that after eleven I should run the cold drink house. But I had enough of that life and was fed up of that. Most of my summer holidays, while I was in school, I spent day and night running that place but no more.

I very politely refused as we respected our father. Usually, it was either his way or the highway. He knew very well that to become a doctor one first had to graduate with Bachelor of Science, and then medical school. He knew that college for B.SC was the whole day and that would not serve his purpose. My hopes and dreams to become a doctor were dashed. My friend Vijay went on to become a doctor, and I was looking for a job.

I checked with all my friends and contacts looking for possibilities of landing a job. With only a basic Matriculation degree, there was a dearth of opportunities and openings. Even a BA graduate had a challenging time to score even a decent clerical job. In spite of initial limitations, I finally got a job, through a friend, as an apprentice in a mechanical shop.

The shop was a large space where old press machines and the likes were brought to the factory. The machines, were dismantled completely to the smallest screws, brushed and then cleaned on a machine. This was run by a fast motor with wire brushes spinning at a very high speed that left the machine parts shining as if new. One had to hold both the large and small parts onto the fast rolling machine, and if one was not careful one could get hurt. Once all parts were good as new, it had to be reassembled.

Somewhat accident prone, it happened to me. I was new and I held the part too long and my hand slipped with the result that I got a deep gash on my pinkie finger which bled profusely. I yelled in pain and the factory supervisor, Mr. Walker an Anglo-Indian gentleman rushed to my aid and held his kerchief on my finger, and later bandaged it after disinfecting it. The scar from the incident is still visible.

The name of the mechanical shop was Hashemboy Jetha after a wealthy Khoja Ismaili gentleman. Sadru his nephew also worked there as an assistant to one of the chief mechanics and used his relationship to the owner to try and boss everyone. The worker did not pay much heed but did not have the guts to say anything either.

One day, I went to the store to pick up a part Sadru was there. He had a heavy part in his hand and kept it on the floor. As the store manager was about to give me the small part, Sadru snatched it from his hand, and pointing to the floor he ordered me to carry the heavy part. After I refused, Sadru was shocked. No one had ever had the courage to refuse him.

We exchanged a volley of words with him using foul language, but I put him in his place. I called him a bastard and explained to him that he could bully everyone but not me. He threatened me by saying that he would be waiting outside after work and I easily accepted the challenge.

Jules was a catholic boy who lived in Love Lane. He was also an apprentice like myself. Since he was more or less like a neighbour, we always accompanied one another to work. We always took the tram from Byculla to Chinchpokli where the factory was located.

The bell rings. It was 5 p.m. and workers are packing their stuff to leave. Jules worries for me and tells me to be careful reminding me that Sadru is older and taller than me. I tell Jules not to worry. I was confident that I could handle the situation as I had learned to box and had worked out on punching bags.

When we came out of the shop, Sadru was waiting. I told myself that this guy is confident that he will knock me out, because I was much shorter than him. I had learned from my boxing training days, that if ever confronted with a stronger opponent, remember to first hit very hard where it hurts the most, then half the battle is won!

I walked ahead with confidence with Jules right behind me. As soon as I approached Sadru, I just gathered my strength and pounded him with a hard punch on his nose. His nose began bleeding and he staggered trying to regain his balance. He grabbed on to my sleeves, but I pushed him aside with another hard sock to his stomach and a hard one to the side of his head. The battle was over, he was sprawled on the floor and could not get up. My shirt was completely ripped apart, and I was partially naked. Workers took Sadru in and gave him first aid.

I never wore an under shirt, so I was naked above the waist. Luckily Jules wore a half sleeve under shirt which he lent me. On the way home the topic of discussion was "The Fight." While coming to work the following day, Jules was worried, and was concerned I might lose my job. Sadru was a relative of the owner after all so it was understood it might be my last day.

As soon as I entered the factory, everybody cheered me on with a huge welcome. Mr. Walker, a serious man who smiled very rarely, walked up to me and softly said, "Good show lad, that bastard deserved to be taught a lesson." Sadru was late to work. He walked in with a bandage on his nose and a black eye. The foreman teased Sadru and told Sadru that it was a shame, a kid had knocked him out. Sadru was not liked by any worker because of his repugnant demeanour and behaviour. From that day on Sadru was no longer arrogant and kept to himself.

Jules and I were working on our machine, when a peon from the main office, which was next to the factory, came to see us telling that the boss was summoning me. Jules suggested to me in a concerned voice that he believed that I was getting fired.

At the office, the secretary pointed me to Mr. Jetha's office. He very swiftly and directly asked why I had beaten his nephew and because of this he should fire me. I told him that was his choice and prerogative, but that Sadru had initiated the fight. After I related everything to him Mr. Jetha was understanding. He told me to return to my work and the next time if I had any problems, I should come directly to him.

As apprentices, we received only one Rupee a day which was sixteen annas. At 11 a.m., we got a fifteen-minute break when we had tea and batata vada, a small snack which cost another four annas. A Hindu restaurant next to the factory made sure we got our tea in time. At the end of the day I was left with eight annas, and then had to pay a small amount for lunch.

For weekends we were not paid. Overall, we roughly earned around twenty Rupees a month. This gave an opportunity to my dad to taunt me. He paid the manager, an illiterate man at our cold drink house Rupees seventy-five a month, while I being educated was earning only Rupees twenty. By now my dad had become a nasty cantankerous old man to the extent that during dinner he would cruelly state that I was eating free food, which he had never said before. He was doing all of this with the hope that I would return to and run the cold drink house.

For the first time I really believed that I must leave the house and venture on my own. Thinking is one thing but doing is another. Night and day, I was racking my brain, but I could not come up with any solution. Despair, pain and agony lasted for a long time then one late night while lying awake, a glimmer of inspirational hope came to me. I knew what I must try.

Granny's Passing On May 13th will always be embedded in my mind. I had just finished high school, and on this day my dear Granny fell ill. This was a person who had never had any sickness all her life, apart from the common cold; she was tough as steel. But age of about age 84, she began complaining of excruciating pain. It was around 8 p.m. and we had finished eating. All of our meals - breakfast, lunch and dinner - were at my granny's house. We only went to our house on the top floor to sleep, never before had she asked anybody to sleep with her but that night she did. She called out to my mum and told her to let me sleep with her.

I was very glad that Granny had chosen me, and I told her not to worry and that I would look after her. I was well-schooled in the anatomy of human beings, and I had just scored 99 percent in Physiology in metric exams. I instinctively knew the pain Granny was suffering from was related to her liver as the discomfort was on her left side. She told me to heat a brick on the primus stove, wrap it up in a towel so as to create a warm compress. When I was a kid she looked after me and now, it was I looking after her.

I did not sleep the whole night while taking care of her. I noticed her looking up and speaking to God. She was silently accepting that it was her time to go and beseeching HIM to take her away peacefully. In the morning, when the whole family came down for breakfast, I told my mum that Granny will not survive till noon as she had been talking to God. I told her that her liver had given up. After breakfast, Dad went to one of his restaurants, and I went to the cold drink house, wondering if Granny will live another day. I prayed that she may go peacefully.

Summer was the most busy time for the cold drink house and as I was busy attending to the customers, around 3 p.m. Haibollah came to me, sobbing that Granny had gone. I asked the manger to take over, and I left with him. We took the tram as it led straight to the cemetery. Fortunately, I was in time for the funeral prayers.

After all the prayer ceremony concluded, three others and myself stepped inside the grave, and placed her body gently, turning the head towards Mecca while sobbing throughout. As I write this, over 65 years later I still cry. Granny was a momin-a holy person- in the true sense of the word.

Our family doctor, who examined her at around 9.30 in the looming, confirmed it was her liver that failed her. I had never met her husband, my grandfather, of whom she used to say that he was a holy person. He never went to any mosque to pray, but he prayed at home, and though he was poor, he helped everybody less fortunate than himself.

Granny used to implore him to go to the mosque, but he would say, "The day I go, you will come to know that I am a believer." One day he became very sick, and according to granny, he began hallucinating. All of a sudden, he addressed the angel of death to go to some lady as it was her time and his time was at eight o'clock. Sure enough, the lady passed away and my grandfather died at p.m.

One night, it dawned on me to apply for a job at the Burmah Shell Refinery. I wanted to know in detail how and where to send my application. I had a Catholic friend who had already applied, and he guided me how to proceed. He told me straight that I did not qualify as the minimum education required was BSC and I was only a matriculate.

What was the harm in applying, I argued and he smiled, shaking his head. Our school knew that many graduated students were bound to be looking for jobs, so they allotted time after school for students who wanted to learn the art of writing a job application. My application letter for a job at the Refinery was good, or at least I thought so.

To my surprise, after about ten days, I received an answer in mail. I was so excited as I read the letter, and to my amazement I was to report to the Refinery for an interview with Mr. Eager, at 10 a.m. The night before I could not sleep and lay awake, praying to God for help.

The Refinery was far away from my house and I had to walk about three miles to the Byculla train station, then ride the train to Sion train station, from where I had to board a bus to the Refinery. It was a tedious journey, but I was young, so it did not bother me too much. I arrived half an hour early to a huge place which resembled a large town. I was amazed and felt lost and wondered helplessly how I was going to find my way to the main office for the interview.

At the gate there was an office, manned by a single person. I showed him the letter and he pointed me to a building to the left and informed me to go to the first floor where interviews were held.

In the waiting room, I found ten other applicants waiting patiently. I sat down and pondered that these guys must be holding degrees, so what I was doing here?

At around quarter to twelve, I was told by Mr. Eager's secretary to go into the office. As I stepped in, I saw a tall, bald but handsome Englishman who looked great in his white shirt and trousers offset with a hunter green silk tie. He had a very kind simile, and I knew right then that the interview would proceed easily.

He spoke softly and told me to be seated. I had an intuitive conviction in my head that it would be easy to speak to him. He went over my application and asked why I had not mentioned my educational qualification. I was relaxed, so I knew I could be funny. I replied if I had I would not be sitting here in front of you. I informed him that I was only a Matriculate. Smiling, with one hand rubbing his ear lobe, he said that he really did not know how he could offer rue the job.

With utmost ease I replied that it was simple; all he had to say was that I was hired. He smiled. I could see he liked me. He smiled, then proceeded to tell me that I was very small in stature. I politely replied that although I was small, but I could do any tough work. There were wore smiles and by then I was completely at ease. I also related to him my life story and my hard work from the age of six, and he began nodding his head, as if he was getting convinced.

He finally asked how old I was, and I told him I was seventeen. He closed his eyes shook his head and informed me that the Refinery rules mandated that any employee must be at least nineteen years of age. I was getting bolder because he was trying to find a way to hire me. I told him here in India they don't have I.D. cards so no one would ever find out my real age.

He smiled and told me that he would take a chance on me but that I should never disappoint him. He shook my hand and told me an appointment letter would soon follow and be sent to me. He added, finally while shaking my hand, that it had been a very interesting and pleasant conversation.

I was placed in the Chemicals and Effluent Unit. Our department had eight very big centrifugal pumps and one very big one; two huge Storage tanks- columns. There was a huge black box like unit completely fireproof. There was no doors or windows, and inside acid sludge was burnt in this large contraption. It had two large wheels like you have on ships.

Large pipes stemming from our unit went to many units like the Distillation Unit, Bitumen plant etc, carrying sulphuric acid, which was used to refine gasoline, kerosine etc. Once the acid was used, it became sludge and it came to our unit to be burnt.

The two large wheels on the black contraption were right in the centre; the left wheel controlling the flow of acid sludge and the right monitoring the flow of fuel. If both were in sync, then the sludge would burn.

The knack was to balance the proportion of the acid and the fuel oil precisely. If they were not in sync, the fuel oil would not be sufficient to burn the sludge whence the fire would extinguish and all the acid sludge would stick to the inner wall of the contraption, and fire would go out. As soon as this happened, you had to increase the fuel oil and the sludge on the wall would catch fire, resulting in a heavy back draft. The fire would come out from the opening around the wheels with a scary force. This sometimes burnt our overalls which we used to extinguish with our heavy-duty gloves.

The refinery maintained all precautions for our safety. Alongside all the sulphuric acid pipes and the pipes with the sludge, there were pipes with fresh running water. If by accident, the pipes carrying acid or sludge leaked, it would fall right on our heads or shoulders. If it hit our heads, it would not be so much of a problem as everyone had to wear heavy duty hats throughout the refinery.

But if the scorching acid fell on our shoulders, the acid would quickly burn the overalls and our bodies. I took extra precaution by wearing thick clothing under my overalls. We were taught that as soon as we heard any drops falling which were inevitable, we would also see smoke arising from the burning overalls. Even if it leaked on our bodies, we had to immediately open the faucet and stand under the water for some time.

Imagine how difficult it was to memorize the names and functions of each and every pipe running to and fro from our plant to each and every corner of the refinery! On top of that was the deafening noise of the centrifugal pumps when powered on, which we also got accustomed to. All this was taught while the refinery was being built.

Finally, the big day of the refinery opening arrived - for the startup - it was a moment everyone was anxiously waiting for. The refinery came to life, and the din of all the plants working was so great that you could hardly hear anyone, unless you shouted. The pressure was not as difficult at our plant compared to other plants where academic qualifications were very important. Conversely someone with only a high school diploma could operate at our plant, albeit with a physically taxing routine.

At this moment, I would like to tell of two incidents before the start-up. On one occasion I was checking the oil gauge of the pump, one of the acid pipes leaked, and to my bad luck it fell straight on my shoulder. I knew it was acid for as soon as it fell within seconds, I could feel the sting on my shoulders, I opened the water faucet immediately and stood under it for around ten minutes. By that time the acid had found its way to my skin. The burn was minimal.

Back in our plant we were preparing to check the final steam flow through pipes and columns. These had very narrow spiral steps. I was the shortest and small so our charge hand, Mr. Gould asked me to climb and check the valve and close it. Before I could check, the steam was on its way from the steam plant and I was surrounded with scorching steam as the valve was not closed.

I could not climb down, I lost my nerves and I was so scared that I could not hear my supervisor shouting "Jump! Jump!" He was a big fellow and I finally jumped straight into his hands, he caught me but the force of my weight coming down was so great that we both fell to the ground.

We were not hurt except he bruised his back and I was red in the face.

All refinery operators were assembled for a demonstration, the fire chief - a chubby fellow who looked exactly like Hardy from Laurel and Hardy - held on to a hose around six inches in diameter or more. For demonstration, a big oil fire was lit; the chief held the hose under his left arm pit and with his right gradually opened the faucet. Foam gushed out with tremendous force, and within minutes the fire was extinguished. Everyone tried and did well for they were older and stronger. Among these guys I looked like a kid. My turn came and I knew this is a task I was ill-equipped to handle.

The foam gushed out of the hose at a tremendous force and it was such a force that I was being pulled from right to left and back. The chief immediately shut the faucet and said, "Alladin, do me a favour just stand back and let the others extinguish the fire." I just did not have the strength to do it. From then on all the operators called me the bacha (meaning kid) of the refinery.

We were two operators in our plant and our responsibilities entailed the following: ensuring that the giant centrifugal pumps ran smoothly, watching the main line regularly; watching the heat meters et al. The most challenging task was maintaining the big black unit, where the acid sludge was burnt. My friends and I took turns, which was extremely taxing to our health and well- being.

Imagine working inside the black room where temperatures reached around 10,000 degrees Fahrenheit. We had to climb up four steps, via a three by three feet platform that could only provide standing room, and which was surrounded by iron rails. One had to continuously monitor the equal flow of the fuel oil with the acid sludge which was next to impossible to achieve.

Almost all plants needed Sulphuric acid for processing all petroleum products including gasoline, kerosine, bitumen etc. All storage tanks were large and we had to every hour on the hour take the measurements of the tank (known as ullaging), means of checking how far the tanks were empty. This was the most hated job by both of us. We had to wear a total head mask which covered our face, goggles, and a snorkel protruding from the mouth and nose. All of this was to protect us from the fumes which rushed up as soon as we opened for taking the ulage. There was a big light above the hatch where we could see the acid bubbling inside. This was done by lowering a metal about six inches long and one inch in diameter with its head tied with a heavy-duty string.

It took great patience and steady hands to slowly let it down just enough to touch the surface of the of the acid in the tank. The measurement was noted on a long sheet which the charge hand on his regular rounds took note of. The worst part was that as soon as the hatch was opened, the fumes which were extremely strong, penetrated through the mask into our nose and our lungs. Two of us who took alternative turns for the operation which was genuinely detrimental and harmful to our health.

We had three rotational shifts of which the morning shift was the best from eight in the morning till four in the afternoon. The next shift was four p.m. to midnight and the toughest was from midnight till eight a.m. As mentioned, it took me two hours to commute which meant I worked ten hours in all rain or shine. The rainy season was the worst with Bombay monsoons with rains measuring around 100 inches in four months.

All plants had cycles, of which ours had two. The responsibility of the burning flare cane under our plant. The flare is a prominent feature of all refineries with a flame burning on the top of a long narrow stack which is an essential part of the plant safety system. Flare stacks are used to combust flammable gases, that are released through pressure relief valves rather than emitting it directly to the atmosphere. I had to cycle to the flare quite a distance from our unit and open the faucet below where condensed water had accumulated.

The canteens made sure that their several of their workers brought tea to the plants. They must have been cycling miles every day from plant to plant. They were always a welcome sight. All operators brought their own lunch, dinner and snacks. You could see all the operators, pouring in from their shifts, carrying their lunch boxes or tiffins.

My sister Meher made sure that when I was ready to leave, my snacks, lunch, or dinner was always packed. Most of the time, Abdullah went to Sarvi restaurant and bought their famous kababs with all the trimmings, and bread from the clay oven. Occasionally, Meher made omelette etc. She really was my favourite sister then as she is now. Being very young and hardworking, I had developed a voracious appetite, which needed constant feeding. There was no break; we had to work right up to the next shift.

I always brought the salary straight to try sister Meher. She kept it in a safe place. Whenever I needed some money, she would give it to me. She was my safe box. Whenever I spent more than I should, she would stop me from spending any more. At the end of the month there was always some money left over.

The measuring of the acid and sludge was gradually taking its toll on me. I was coughing more and more every day. I checked with our family physician, Dr. Dongaji who had looked after us from the day we were born, he advised me strongly to resign from the refinery job, for he knew the fumes of the sulphuric acid could make me sick.

After seven months, I resigned with great reluctance as for a matriculate Rupees 125 a month and overtime, if one shift operator could not make it, I had to cover for him which made me work sixteen hours straight without a break. That brought me a very good overtime pay. I could never earn so much with a clerical job.

Once again, I was jobless and at the mercy of my dad. But by now he had calmed down. He saw that I was a determined kid, who was prepared to handle any hard work. So, he told me nicely - which was novel for him - to take over the cold drink house. He was prepared to match what I had been earning. I always respected my dad, so I very politely told him that the salary was not the issue, but I was fed up of working in restaurants. I also told him that I was working from the age of six and I had enough of that life.

Before I had resigned from my refinery job, on one occasion returning from my morning shift Rubab Aunty was waiting for rue at our home. She was chatting about we with my mum. As soon as she saw me, she hugged rue, to soften the ensuing shock. She softly told rue the shocking news, Najafi aunty had taken Nosrat to Karachi. My mum too tried to console me, to no avail. She knew how much I loved Nosrat, she kept on saying marriage is made in heaven, and that someday I will find someone deserving.

Ezzat always told me about her mum's plans to get Nosrat married to a rich man in Karachi. I came to know later he was much older. I do not know how old for I had never met this lucky man. I took solace in the thought that he must be a good man and he will take good care of Nosrat.

I felt I had to go to Karachi. But how? I just wanted to call her and ask what happened to the vows we had taken at Juhu Beach. After that closure, I would try and forget her as time and patience heals all wounds. It was easy to think this way but convincing the heart is another thing altogether.

Out of the blue, 1 was finally going to Karachi after all, hoping that I would get a chance to talk to Nosrat. To be continued.

Cecilia

After work, we used to stand at the gate of our compound fooling around and looking at girls passing by. They did not seem to mind as they would smile and wave as they passed on. One evening I saw a very pretty girl dressed in a, slightly transparent frock with a lovely petticoat visible through the frock; a sight to behold! I asked the boys how come I had never seen her before.

Sadru said he had already seen her a couple of times, accompanied with, a kind of an ugly woman (not a nice thing to say but we are teen aged and did not any better). He added maybe she was her ayah (maid). They used to take the shortcut through our compound to go to Love Lane. The narrow passage which lead to Love Lane was next to my granny's house. My mum and granny used to sit on a large cot outside her house. I told Sadru, tonight I will ask my mum if she had seen them.

Yes, my mum had seen them. She described the girl as sad looking and the poor woman with her as rather ugly, immediately adding may God forgive her for saying so. After a couple of days, the same girl was passing by alone, from the across the road where we were standing at our main compound gate. I asked the boys to wish me good luck before I went after her.

She was a few steps ahead as I tried catching up with her and noticed her beauty up close for the first time. She had straight beautiful silky hair right up to her lower back and iron the looks of it she took great car e of it. She was also preciously stylish for her age and was self-aware that she was something special which one could assess in the way she walked and carried herself.

I thought to myself that this pretty and confident girl would be a very hard catch.

I walked alongside her and introduced myself. I knew she was the type of a girl who loved praises, so I fed her ego and told her that she was very pretty, and that I wanted to be her friend. I thought I was also quite nice looking, and I was sure we could get together.

Without turning her head, she coyly said her name was Cecilia and she knew I was interested in her and that frankly she was also interested in me.

Without showing her my feelings, I said to myself, "Yes!" And then, I asked her to go out for tea and samosas so we could get to know one another better.

She excused herself as she was on her way to see one of her relatives. She was not shy and said we could meet the next day same time. I had succeeded and when I told the boys they jokingly said, "You lucky bastard you score all the time." We fooled around had tea in the Irani restaurant next to our compound and went home. My mum knew about all my girlfriends and when I told her about Cecilia, she said, "I am sure you will break her heart too."

The following day I put together my smartest outfit and waited for her at the gate. She finally came, smiled and gave he her hand. I took it and then I put it around her waist. Although she always had an air of reserve and pride, to my pleasant surprise, she too put her hand around my waist, and we were already lovebirds. In those days, it was common to see couples walking around with their arias around their partners.

After tea and snacks we walked, towards Mazgaon Hills Gardens, and started ascending the pathway which was not too steep. It led to a space of beautiful gardens with all kinds of tropical plants. It was an expansive area and from its peak you could see the Mazgaon Docks. Both young and old would visit this vista because it offered everybody something to relax, after a hard day's work.

Children could play in the sand, and both young and elderly couples walked taking in the lush greenery and the cool breeze. There were many benches all around and people relaxed and really enjoyed their selves. Best of all there was no entrance fee.

Along the winding path there were some secluded spots here and there where one could spot couples like us sitting on benches; kissing; holding hands, and enjoying blissful hours, before they went back to their very small living quarters. I picked the most secluded spot which very few people used. So here, Cecilia and I had our first kiss and making out, and all the things which teenagers do. But as I mentioned before, I NEVER ever went too far by taking any girl's honour.

Cecilia's house was close to our compound. From the gate on the right-hand side there was an alley which ended up in a cull de sac. The entrance of the building led to an open space. There was another building inside and she lived on the top floor. Nesbit bridge was just outside our compound and the alley was on its right side. The top of the bridge had a small stairway leading down to the building where Cecilia lived. From the top of the bridge one could see the window of her house. It was a convenient short cut for all the tenants living in that building.

Whenever l reached the top, l used to loudly whistle the famous tune, "Cherry Pink and Apple Blossom White". Cecilia would come to the window wave and then cone out. We always met at the top of the bridge and now we also had an additional hide out where we could romance. The hide out was the Byculiah railway grounds. From the entrance, a small path led onto a compound. Opposite the compound, were rail lines, and occasionally one could see trains passing by.

There was a large tree and we used to sit on the raised cement seat around it. We used to go there after sunset in the evening, for after that no on one cane there. It used to be dark as there were no lights, a good place to romance and we had the place to ourselves. Around 8 p.m., I used to walk her to staircase of the bridge, checked that there was no one around, kiss her good night and then she would go home. This place and Mazgaon Hills Garden became our regular romancing spot.

St Mary School, in later years, had begun night school from five in the evening to eight p.m. All the students were hooligans and loafers with a few exceptions. Before and after school, they sat on the iron railings which was right on top of the alley of the Nesbit Bridge, and passed dirty remarks to girls who happened to be alone and passing by. Three of these bad boys were the worst kind, who thought they could get away with anything, or so they thought.

I had no knowledge that this trio had found out about Cecilia's routine with me. They never tried anything with her because I was always with her and they were cowards. One horrible day though, it so happened that when we came out of the Byculla grounds, my friends were waiting for me. They knew about our hideout. So, they were waiting outside the grounds.

Sadru told me that he had free movie tickets for the last show and the movie was starting at 9 p.m. I asked Cecilia if she could go home alone from there and she told me not to worry. Stupid of me it would have taken at most ten minutes to reach her, but when things are meant to happen, they happen.

After the movie, around midnight I and my friends were in the compound where we sat on the cool marble seats surrounding the fountain. We were young and full of energy and passed our time till around two past midnight, and then went home.

Most days after dinner, I would go to Sanjivan, a friend of mine happened to live on the first-floor opposite to Cecilia's house. From my friend's window I had a clear view of Cecilia's room window. As usual, I whistled our tune and she would come to the window. Sanjivan and I used to go for a walk after dinner.

One night I was walking towards Sanjivan's house when a couple of good kids from night school, caught me at the gate and gave me the ugly news.

On the movie night when I had asked her to go by herself, the three hooligans had tried to molest Cecilia, right next to the steps of the bridge. With great difficulty, she freed herself and went home crying. I suddenly turned into a mad man and was not myself. My eyes became red-shot, for a moment my mind went blank. Where could I find those bastards, I kept repeating to myself with my hands on my head trying to cool down and ponder where I could find them.

The kids told me the three thugs had just gone to Byculla near Spencer Road. I hurried to Sanjivan's home and told him of the incident and told him to hurry before I lost them. We took the usual route, and luckily, we found the three loafers harassing and stealing from a road vendor selling chana batata (cooked chickpeas with potatoes, served in small cup with chutney).

This gang always hung out together. The ringleader was a dark, strong, and tall boy. I recognized them and just walked up to them without any warning and spun the tall boy and landed a very hard punch to his nose which began bleeding on his shirt. The two other cowardly boys just ran away. I told him, "Stay away from my girl or else I will kill you." He said he would not forget this and he would see me later. I told him, "Any day. And come alone if you are not a coward." Sanjivan was standing on guard his eyes on the other two.

The next day Cecilia and I went to Mazgaon Hills Gardens, one of our love spots, the other being Byculla grounds. I told her not to worry as those cowards would never try to hurt her again. While I was telling her about the fight, she all of a sudden hugged me so hard with love that I felt her deep gratitude. The same kids who had told me about the molestation, informed me that the gang leader I had beaten up had gathered his supporters from school, and would be coming to the grounds to seek revenge. He was a coward and that is why he needed support.

I was not about to back down. On the ground floor of Cecilia's building, facing the compound, lived Ronnie, with his sister and brother-in-law, Pat, a good friend of mine. He was tough as they come. Another very good friend was Bobby Lillywhite, Pat's brother who was married to Buddu. Ronnie was always working out on Roman Rings. I asked him if he would accompany me and keep an eye on Cecilia when we were in the compound as we were not about to cancel our date for anything. Above all, the thug would think I got scared.

Ronnie was eager to join us and so was Zia Mahmoud's younger brother with two hockey sticks. I just wanted them to be my back-up. Cecilia pleaded we should not go but I convinced her that I would never let anything happen to her. I comforted her by telling her that Ronnie and Zia were standing at the gate, and as soon as they saw them coming they would come inside and be ready for action. We three could take their whole gang out.

Soon, about 20 of the gang leader's cronies and suckers poured into the grounds. As soon as they approached rue, I showed them the palm of my had and in a commanding voice told them all to halt right there. I told the leader I had punched a deal: If he wanted to fight me on a one-to-one basis we should get on with it and if he wanted to fight with his gang, because he was a coward, that was also okay for we three can beat the hell out of them.

The whole motley crowd did not have the guts and as soon as they heard me, I could see fear in their eyes. The leader too got scared and said, "I am not here to fight but just needed an apology." I reminded him that he was the coward who molested a girl, and I would never apologize. He began mumbling with his head down, ashamed to face his gang, and they all walked away. My darling Cecilia who was hiding behind the tree came out with a sigh of relief and suggested I could have apologized because all the while her heart was in her mouth and she could not breathe. All is well that ends well.

Going back to Bobby, he was an Anglo-Indian whose father, an Englishman, had settled in Bombay and married a Indian woman. Bobby lived in a tiny one-room apartment but had a huge heart and was a gem of a guy. He was married to an Indian girl Budoo, and they had one daughter. Both Bobby and his brother worked at the Kodak factory and lived in the same building.

I could go to Bobby's house any time I wanted and was always welcomed. I could open the chatti (cooking vessel), and just eat whatever was cooked - that's what I meant by him having a big heart, although poor.

On Sundays, a couple of friends along with Bobby went to a posh place like Colaba to listen to jazz and '50s Rock 'n' Roll on juke box. You put four annas (16 Anna's made a Rupee) in a slot of the juke box and while the music played we enjoyed eating omelettes with toast and Heinz ketchup end- noted with delicious piping hot tea which we all really enjoyed. I still fondly remember every moment of those amazing days.

When Bobby immigrated to Australia, I was so lost specially on Sundays, but the rest of us continued to meet but we missed him and kept on telling each other that we wished Bobby was still here. Immediately after Bobby's departure to Australia, I, too, had decided to move to Karachi.

But can you believe it, after I left, Ronnie married Cecilia, although he knew about our love affair. What a sport!

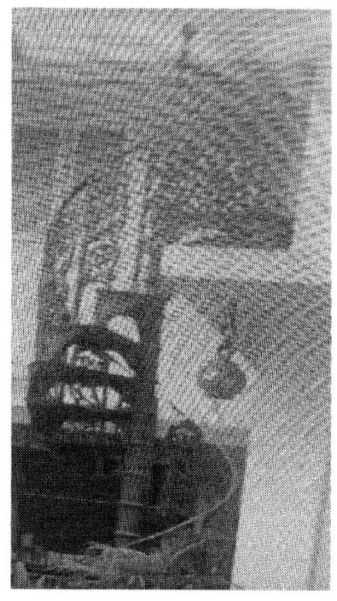

Spiral Staircase

11 Years Old

15 Years old

17 Years Old

50's Sister Firouze, Meher, Juju, Gulshehkar and Sheroo

1956 Juhu Beach – Sis, Bibi, Meher and Zohra

Abu Padamsee

Zahara Khaleh and Grand Kids

Agahall compound – Born here

Agahall

Alimohamd, Padamsee our group scout master

Compound Boys

Archi Babas daughter Qamar and sis Omeh Habibeh

Archie Baba

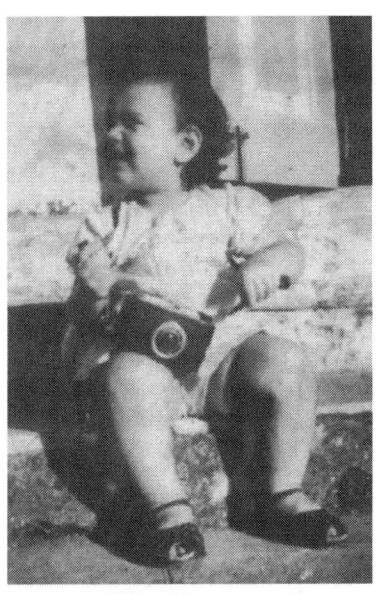

Baby Qamar

Banglore Mum, Bibi, Meher and Farrokh

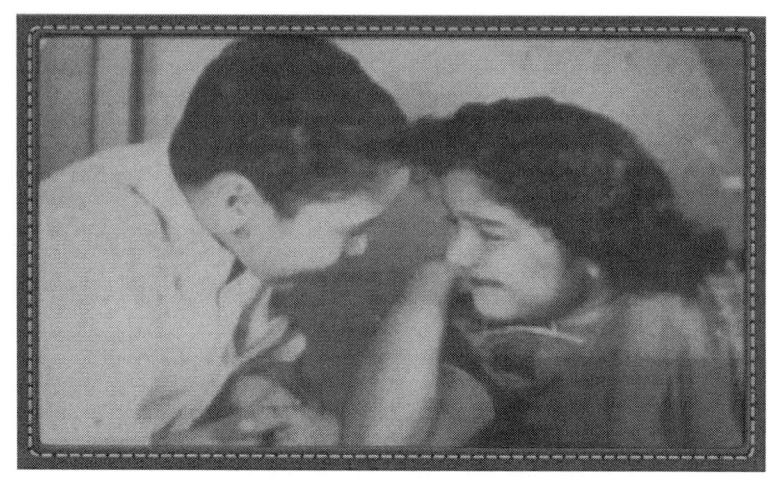

Salehmuhammad & Razia – Childhood friends

Bombay swimming pool – 1955

Brother Ghulam Hussein

Boxing with Sadru

Bro-in-law Jimmy, Bobby, Self and Imani

Brother Farrokh – 1970's

Brother Ghulam Hussein, Firouze, Meher, Omeh, Farrokh

Cycling with Osborne and Reuben

Cycling 100 miles with Reuben and Ozborne

Dolly Aunty and kids

Fatu dancing – Ghulam, Zohra, Self and Joginder

Firouze, 3 children and Meher

Firouze and Meher

Firouze and Basanti

Girlfriend Cecelia – 1955

Hadi Kizilbash

Granny

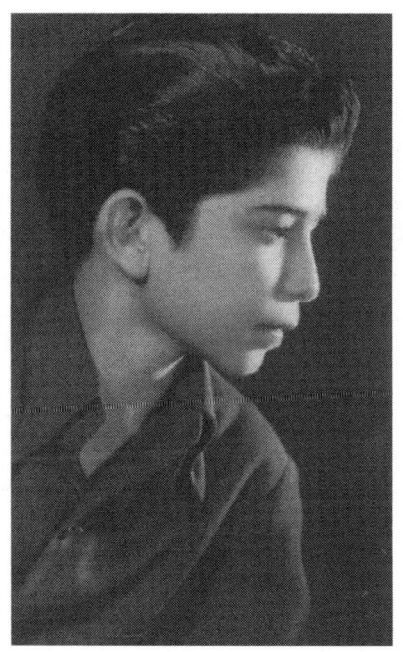

Headshot for film Shabistan

Bibi Tela

Ismail Padamsee – Our scout master

Ghulam Hussein, his girl Zohra, Self and girlfriend Joginder

Lighted gate – Agahall

Marzieh Khaleh & Children

Mehdi and Hadi

Mother & Nader, Juju, Malik and Anwar

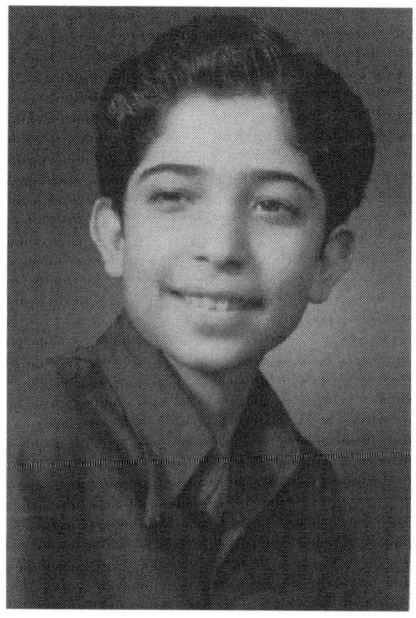

My headshot for film – 12 years old

My mother Ruqiyyeh

Nader and Juju

Nader and Juju

Juju, Nader, Malik and Anwar

Niece Juju

Nokoo

Ruda, Aunty and Papoli

Sanjivan

Sister Firouze

Sister Meher in slacks – 1955

Self – 1955

Sister Meher with girlfriend Gubo

Sister Bibi, Tela, Abdulla, Zahra and Fatima

Sisters Firouze and Meher

Uncle Ali Khan leading winner

Uncle Ali Khan – Maharaja Cup for his horse

Uncle Sohrab Khan

Uncle Ali Khan in Bangalore

With Babu Bhai and Noordin – 1960's

Zohra, Bibi, Tela, Meher, Shamsi – Juhu Beach

Foreword & Edited by Zurain Imam (Karachi Pakistan)

The desire and dedication to pen one's memoirs in the autumn of one's life - one filled with upheavals, struggles, adventures, and success- requires great courage; fortitude; a perennially youthful (and mischievous) spirit and a kind heart. These qualities are the very reason why I was delighted and agreed to help Alladin Kamria — known to me as Ali Uncle-edit his multi- volume reminisces of his eventful life. Ali Uncle is family to me. In the roaring late '50s he was "adopted" by the Imam brothers - my paternal uncles- when he met them in Karachi and developed a specially close relationship with my father, M. Zaffar Imam (Late). There are countless sepia photographs in our family archives of the two of them frolicking and dancing at nightclubs with glamorous women or posing casually at the beach and other locales.

This first volume (Vol. 1) of "Alladin's Magical Memoirs" recounts the memoirist's early years growing up in Bombay with an intimate introduction to his family and relationships with school friends and work colleagues; some of which have been sustained for over 60 years; the young and ambitious teenager working at his father's restaurant; squabbles with school bullies; finding professional independence working at a factory; catching the infectious acting bug and performing on stage and on-screen and of course his myriad love affairs and breaking of hearts including a tribute to "the love of his life." In a Simple stream of consciousness writing style, Alladin Kamria poignantly recollects his earliest memories which formed the genesis and foundation of the gentleman he has become, one who has still kept his "naughty" inner child indubitably alive.

Front cover design – By my son-in-law Dan Beers

Volume 2

Ever since I can remember I have always thanked God and been grateful for all the blessings that HE has showered upon me. If and when some door shut on me, miraculously another would open and prevail. One day Abbas Moraj, who lived in Karachi and would often travel to Bombay to meet his family dropped in to see us at our home.

I had learned from his previous visits that he owned a shipping charter company in Karachi. I myself did not know ABCs of shipping. The only exposure I had to maritime life was when I once boarded a merchant ship, docked in one of Bombay's ports, whose captain was my best friend Horace's elder brother.

Horace was a talented singer and guitarist who lived on the top floor of St Mary's school compound which only featured two houses; one which Horace's family occupied, and the other inhabited by Hashim Jalali and his wife, Barbara. In the evenings, Horace and I would wander to Spencer Lane, which was a few minutes' walk from our homes. We sang only American songs accompanied by Horace strumming on his guitar.

Horace and I decided to go visit his brother on the ship. Once there, we saw snacks and beer laid out invitingly on the table. I shyly admitted that hitherto I had never touched or tasted alcohol in my entire life. The captain smiled and told me he would concoct a "Shandy". I wondered what that was as I watched him pour half a bottle of beer and mix it with Seven Up.

Slowly sipping it, I immediately loved the slightly bittersweet fizzy cocktail. But as we got up to leave, I did feel a little light-headed. That was my first ever experience with an alcoholic drink. I liked it so much that whenever I went to a party, I would enjoy the shandy, by now I was used to it and never felt light- headed.

While Mr. Abbas Moraj was enjoying his tea and conversing with my mother, a crazy yet possible notion entered my head. I was cautiously optimistic that my proposed plan might just work out. I approached Abbas Bhai and told him that I was unemployed for the past few months after resigning from my job at the refineries and could he please possibly take me to Karachi with him.

I knew he was aware that I did not know head or tails about shipping. He closed his eyes and while rubbing his forehead - thinking - meanwhile I was on pins and needles - but thankfully he asked me if I could type to which I eagerly replied that I could indeed. As luck would have it, during the past few months I had taken a course in typing, encouraged only by my sister Bibi Tela, who herself was an accomplished stenographer.

Again, Abbas Bhai shut his eyes and began rubbing his forehead in deep thought. I was pretty sure he was ruminating on how he could utilize me as a typist. After a few moments, he looked towards my mother, and asked her if she would allow me to go to Karachi.

It took a lot of pleading and coaxing on my part before she reluctantly gave me permission to go to Karachi with Abbas Bhai. She made him promise that he would take good care of me. I was ecstatic and immediately hugged my mother, who was already crying, and then Abbas Bhai.

My father continued his daily routine of going to the restaurants in the morning and returning home around midnight. When my mum told him about my job in Karachi that night, he smiled, shook his head and proclaimed that I was after all his son and like him, he understood that I too wanted to venture out on my own and explore life's opportunities.

As soon as Abbas Bhai returned to Karachi, he made arrangements for my impending trip. Within about ten days, I received in mail a second-class ticket on a freight ship along with some Pakistani Rupees for when I landed at Karachi port to help me proceed to the address, he had included in the mail.

My darling mum, out of her daily house expenses, saved some money for my trip. She bought a small tin trunk for my clothes which consisted of three pairs of pants with matching shirts: a belt, three pairs of socks, two pyjamas, and a green bush shirt, which I still own, after over sixty years. I still wear it occasionally, once or twice every summer so as not to wear it out. I have maintained my body and it still fits.

My total belongings consisted of one canvas bed roll with a thin mattress: a small pillow and two bed sheets. My youngest brother Farrokh loved me very much and looked up to me for inspiration for everything, from school and acting to flirting with girls. On the day of my departure, Farrokh went outside the compound to fetch a taxi for my ride to the docks.

Once the luggage was loaded, I got into the taxi, and Farrokh began crying. As my taxi drove off, I kept waving to him from the rear window. At this point, Farrokh was sobbing inconsolably. As I write this my eyes still well up with tears after over 60 years.

When I arrived at the port, I was guided by the porter who carried by scanty luggage to customs from where we were ushered, through a line alongside the ship. Everyone embarked onto the vessel in a single line. I showed my ticket to the steward who led me to my cabin at the top deck of the ship. I released a sigh of relief as I was exhausted and threw myself on the narrow bed attached to the side wall.

There were only four cabins on the ship. The rest of the passengers had deck tickets and slept all sprawled out on the deck nestled in their own bedding. My next-door cabin was inhabited by a

Pakistani boy who was returning to Karachi after a visit to Bombay.

One day after lunch I approached him and introduced myself. His name was Rauf and he was a jovial fellow like myself and we enjoyed each other's company.

His company made the trip less boring. Rauf was my very first Pakistani friend.

I had set sail and ventured out to a new country of which I knew absolutely nothing about. I knew it was a Muslim republic formed after the Partition. That's all the knowledge I had. Furthermore, the only Karachi residents I knew were Abbas Bhai and now Rauf.

I suddenly felt a wave of apprehension and fear which increased my heart rate. I was now alone in a cabin and feeling lonely as I had grown up with seven siblings and was used to company. But Rauf and I were spending more and more time together.

When I sensed that he had taken a liking to me, I asked him if we could meet sometimes in Karachi as I would be totally new in the city. Rauf gave me his card and I was somewhat assured that I at least had somebody to contact.

The ship finally arrived at a port known as Gwadar and the ship crew started to offload goods. On the wharf the only people you could see loading carts and lorries with the offloaded goods, otherwise the land was barren as far as I could see from the ship. This was way back in the 1950s. Now, believe Gwadar has been transformed into a beautiful and bustling city.

It took us an additional eight hours to sail and we reached the city of Karachi around eleven in the morning. Gradually passengers disembarked. Rauf met his mother, and he bid me farewell and left.

Fear and loneliness once again enveloped me, and I felt helpless and lost. I was reminded how my father must have felt when he first landed at the docks in Bombay traveling alone from Iran, feeling lost and lonely. Every possible experience my dad must have faced dashed in front of me as I found myself in a similar situation.

Abbas Bhai was not there to pick me up from the port. I was to proceed instead alone to a hotel in Bolton Market. I mustered enough courage and told myself to stop wallowing in self-pity. I looked around for transport and saw a line of motor rickshaws to my right, loading passengers. I walked up to one and told him to take me to Bolton Market.

While riding, I looked around and realised that compared to Bombay, Karachi appeared to look like a village. I saw large, long carts with loaded goods being drawn by camels from the port; and carts with lesser goods being pulled by donkeys. I was also overwhelmed to see scrawny individuals, thin to their bones hand- pulling the carts - this was the same in India.

The crossroads did not have traffic lights and the bustling traffic was instead guided by traffic police standing on a solid wooden block. I was very impressed by the traffic policeman who was very smartly dressed, like the 'sepoys' from the time of the British Raj. He wore a clean white shirt, khaki short pants and socks right up to his calves.

The best part of his uniform was a cone-shaped cap, with a beautiful turban tied around it. The turban was topped by a segment, shaped like a Japanese geisha's fan. I must reiterate that I was really very impressed and mesmerized.

If one hand of the police stopped the traffic coming from one direction, the other arm would simultaneously swing around, and almost in a robotic motion signal the opposite traffic rush to move ahead. I could see the traffic police taking pride in his duty.

On one crossroad I saw the camel cart was approaching only a few feet from the intersection when the police signalled the camel's owner to halt. Well, camels don't have in-built brakes to stop quickly. The camel was obviously much taller than the traffic police standing on the wooden block so by the time the camel came to a sudden stop his head was literally right on top of police's head; an amazing scene to observe indeed!

I finally arrived at my destination and my heart sank. Had the rickshaw driver brought me to the wrong place? He assured me that I was in the right place pointing to the hotel sign. The individuals who were lurking around this area looked repugnant and sent shivers throughput my body and cold sweat dripped down my spine.

I went to the hotel's restaurant cashier and asked him about my room. He pointed to a small outside staircase. My room number was four and I climbed the stairs, dragging my luggage with me.

The corridor was dark, and it took a few seconds for my eyes to adjust. I opened the door lock and peeked into a very dark dungeon.

This is no exaggeration because even though there was bright sunshine outside, the room was dingy and dungeon-like for there were no windows. A small bulb with lowest voltage lit the room just enough for me to see only four steps in front of me. A small spring bed filled the small room with a dirty mattress, pillow and bed sheet.

A tiny bedside table stood alone, on which I placed my traveller's clock. But the most frightening aspect was right in the centre of the room. There was the gaping hole which was about ten inches in diametre. You could see right down into the restaurant and watch diners eating which made my mouth water as my last meal had been on the ship.

I did not dare to go down to the restaurant as almost all the customers were fierce-looking with oversized moustaches and beards; some of them with daggers; these being Pathans from Afghanistan. They looked scary because this was the first time, I had been thrown into such a situation.

How could Abbas Bhai bring me here! But again he too was staying here and it was hardly five minutes' walk from the hotel to Muhamadi House. Abbas Bhai arrived around nine p.m., knocked on the door, and I was relieved to see his familiar, friendly face.

He was a practical man who did not believe in pleasantries. He simply asked me about the trip and gave me directions to the office and went to his room. Anyone staying in this dungeon- like room would feel as I did. I began crying, wondering how long I would have to endure the misery of this hotel.

For company, I had bugs feasting on my blood. While I scratched, my brain kept wondering if I should have stayed in the comfort of my home in Bombay. But I had learnt lessons from my dad about experiencing and bearing with situations but this particular one truly intimidated me.

I had assured faith in God and would not lose hope. HE had always taken care of me and I should not lose the test of having patience and fortitude. My granny always said those who are constant in their prayers and patience will eventually come out of any difficulty. This thought renewed my courage and while praying I finally fell asleep.

My small clock alarm woke me up at eight a.m. Outside the room, there was a small wash basin where I cleaned up. I got dressed up in my room to go to office. I had never worked in any office in my entire life. Once I had an opportunity to work in a posh office of Stanvac Oil Co in Bombay. I got an appointment for the interview, which was arranged by one of my girlfriends, Shamsi whose uncle was the Managing Director of Stanvac. I got the preferential treatment but was not hired for the job as I was not old enough.

The walk to Muhammadi House was hardly five minutes, from the hotel. A small alley led to the backside of the building, and a few steps away was the lift which took me to the fifth floor where Maritime Agency had their offices.

I reached the office and the door was already open. A Pathan was standing next to it. I asked him about wanting to see Mr. Mooraj, and he pointed to a room a little afar.

Right inside the office to the right was a glass cabinet which was the office of Mr. Wali Imam, with its elegant table and chairs. He was partner and Chief Administrator, and everyone was scared of him. Then there was a long table sat the employees with open ledgers in front of them.

Outside Mr. Wali Imam's office, on a small office table sat the CPA whose name was Mr. Jaffri. Right next him was Mr. Wajid, the bookkeeper. I walked slowly through the off, glancing at each person, and to my relief my eyes fell on Abbas Bhai.

It was a large room but only three persons occupied it.

The office was larger than Mr. Wali Imam's. To the right was Mr. Afzal Imam, the brains behind the shipping agency. He was giving instructions to Mr. Khokar, the shipping manager seated right opposite him. Abbas Bhai occupied a small table next to Mr. Afzal Imam. He got up and introduced me to Afzal who received me with kindness and to Khokar.

Just outside their office was the typist Naseem, and I got a tiny table next to him. There was not much to do. But Abbas Bhai was non-stop busy on the phone. I soon found out that Abbas Bhai was sharing the small place in Maritime, and his main business was chartering ships. I believe he shared a small part of his profits with Maritime Agency.

I was getting bored doing nothing, so I introduced myself to Naseem, and all other employees including Mr. Jaffri, Wajid, Razak,

Hassan, Hamid mamoo and Zaffar Imam. Later I found out that Zaffar was the youngest of the five Imam brothers. The oldest was Shahlda Imam, then Wali Imam, Afzal, Mazahar, and Zaffar.

On the first floor was a restaurant, catering to the whole building including our office, where employees went for lunch. Just before lunch Abbas Bhai came out and gave me ten Rupees which was for my lunch and dinner. I was very hungry and had a two eggs omelettes and tea -that was actually my breakfast and lunch.

Everyone was very kind, specially Mazhar, Zaffar, and Hamid mamoo. Zaffar told me kindly to sit next to him. This made me feel like I was already one of them: a very good feeling indeed, especially after the night alone in the dungeon.

At five p.m. everyone was preparing to leave and go home. Abbas Bhai reminded me briefly that office started at eight a.m. and then he left. He was a man of very few words. He preferred his brains to work more than his tongue. The thought of returning to the dungeon swiftly erased all the good feelings I had experienced throughout the day.

I asked Zaffar to go down with me to the restaurant, I bought a sandwich for my dinner. Once I was in the hotel, I would never risk coming down. It was close to six p.m. and I was alone in my dingy room with nothing to do, nothing to even read made me anxious. (Even if I had a book how would I read it in that very dim light?)

Solitude offers an opportunity to reflect. I thought that the rug was being pulled out from under me, and the roof was caving in. I felt the happy days were gone, and I was embroiled in a cold and harsh world. I mustered courage and uttered "what the heck!" and went down. What was the worst that could happen? I was a scrapper; I could defend myself.

Immediately, an incident from my time in Bombay came rushing into my mind. Just outside our compound after the tailor's shop, to the right there was a billiard saloon. The marker who worked there was a retired Anglo-Indian army major, a poor chap who could not make ends meet.

Both my brothers Ghulam Hussein and Saifudin were good snooker players. Saifu was not allowed to step in there as he was still too young. But whenever he could, he would sneak his way into the saloon. Since there was only one table, one had to ask the marker to put the initial of the person reserving the table. He would write the initial of the person reserving the table on a black slate hanging on the wall.

Saifu asked the marker to put his name, and he wrote a big 'S' on the slate with white chalk. I was in the compound when I saw Mahmoud running towards me. He was yelling to hurry and rush to the saloon, and save Saifu from a fight with Sangin, who was older than us and well-built. He was from Badakshan.

Quite a few of them - all Ismaili immigrants — had settled down in our compound. I rushed in the saloon and asked what the problem was. The marker explained the situation. It was Saifu's turn and not Sangin as the latter was falsely claiming that the 'S' stood for his name. I ordered the marker to set up the table. I was going to have a game with my brother.

Sangin was taller than us. Saifu knew in the first place he was not supposed to be in a billiard saloon; he knew I was now going to get into a fight with Sangin. He quickly hugged me, tried to apologise and begged for us to go home. If I had backed down, these immigrants would think we Iranians, like the Khoja Ismailies in the compound, were weak and would try to push their way around us in the compound. That could never, ever happen.

Sangin and his fellow friends had learnt some English, and he told me to F@#k off. That was enough for me to spring into action. I was in an awkward position to throw the first punch. My brother was hugging me and pleading to let go. The only opening I saw was at the side of my brother's head. I landed a straight right jab and freed myself from Said's embrace.

Sangin picked up the billiard cue rest (enabling players to reach the cue ball out of reach) and from its metal side, landed a hard blow to my head. I began bleeding profusely and started to wobble. I caught the side of the table to regain my balance. I woke up and kicked Sangin with all my might in his groin. He doubled down in pain, and the final blow was a hard-right cross to his face. He was down. The fight was over.

As soon as Sadru, my boxer friend, heard about the incident, he came rushing to my aid. When he saw me bleeding, he immediately took me to the police station, which was close to our house. The station was at the crossroads of Love Lane and Byculla.

The inspector in charge recognised Sadru as soon as we stepped in. Sadru boxed for the Police Union and he was the undefeated champ. We lodged a complaint against Sangin to be on the safe side. Sangin's testicles were swollen and he was in pain.

Back to present

I decided to go down for a stroll on what I remember as bustling Bunder Road. The alleys were full of dry fruits vendors and others selling their produce. I was glad I came out as I began to feel normal again. I spotted a decent restaurant, went in for a cup of tea. My heart started setting in peace along with the sun as I walked back to the hotel.

The next morning, I was the first one to arrive at the office. The only other person there was the Layla Pathan who recognized me and ushered me in. I asked him to order some tea for me which he did from the restaurant down below. By the time I finished my tea, other staff members began coming, greeting me and each other with salaams. However, this seemed to be yet another boring day with nothing to do.

Soon to my surprise, Abbas Bhai gave me a hand-written letter and told me to type it out. I returned it to him in five minutes and he was pleased to see my neat and accurate typing. That would be the first and last letter I ever typed in this office.

Before the day was over, I was introduced to Mr. Wali Imam. He was quite nice and inquired from me how I was liking his hometown of Karachi. I asked him if I should be honest and he assured me with a smile. I then told him brazenly that I thought Karachi was like a village compared to Bombay. He smiled agreeably but insisted Karachi was really not a village.

After a couple of days Abbas Bhai handed me an envelope with my first month's salary. He told me he would be away for a long time and that he had spoken to Afzal and from the next day I would begin my apprenticeship under Hamid who would train me to become a shipping clerk.

That was the best news ever! At least I would be busy and learn a new set of skills. Abbas Bhai reassured me further by saying that Afzal was very close to him and would look after me if I had any problems. I opened the salary envelope and found 125 Rupees. I could not take all this money with me so for safety sake I gave 120 Rupees to Wajid the bookkeeper who also handled the petty cash in the office.

Every day I felt happy and content. Hamid mamoo, (Urdu for uncle) showed me the first steps to enter into the log the ships entering and leaving the ports, as well as entering the details of the cargo loaded and off−loaded daily. Hamid mamoo was the most soft spoken and kindest person I had ever met in my life. It was so easy to work under his guidance and tutelage. Additionally, he had liked me from day one.

The restaurant always sent tea to us on a tray with a kettle, a sugar bowl, milk and tea. He always asked for two cups as he always shared his tea with me and also accompanying some snacks. I was eternally thankful to him.

My seat was between Hamid mamoo and Zaffar. To his right sat Mazhar sahab, who handled all the shipping activities in East Pakistan (now Bangladesh).

Now that I was open and free with all of them, - all very friendly - I asked Hamid mamoo, if I could use the phone to call a friend. He had a look of surprise on his face and asked how come I had already found a friend in Karachi as I had hardly been there a week. I told him about Rauf who I had met on the ship. I took out Rauf's card and dialled his number. Rauf was really surprised and happy to hear from me.

After exchanges of pleasantries, I told Rauf about the predicament of my hotel room and how I would go crazy if I continued staying there. I told him to ask his Christian friends to look around for any family who were prepared to take me in as their paying houseguest. My experience in Bombay had been Christian families who took in boarders usually treated them like family members and charged them a reasonable monthly fee in exchange for boarding and lodging.

Rauf said he would try his best as he had many friends, and somebody was bound to find a place for me. Rauf told me to call him back in a week and he hoped to have some good news for me by then. He sympathized with me after he found out the room was no less than a dungeon.

Meanwhile the days were great at the office. Zaffar and Mazhar sahab, while hearing my story as I was speaking to Rauf, were shocked as to how Abbas Bhai had arranged such shabby quarters for me. I stood up for Abbas Bhai and explained to them that my apartment was in close proximity to the office, and besides Abbas Bhai also lived in the same hotel although his room was of course quite brighter and large.

The two Imams were helpless themselves- otherwise they would help me - as the themselves stayed with Shaida Imam the eldest of the Imam brothers whom I had not yet met.

Some good came out of my phone conversation as Zaffar and Mazhar sahab began sharing their food and drinks with me. That was a very sweet gesture on their part and helped me to save some money. Hamid mamoo or either Zaffar or Mazhar sahb took care of breakfast and lunch. This group had become like family, so I was not missing my own family as much. But of course, I missed my mum she was truly the best. It's undoubtably true that no one - absolutely no one - can take the place of a mother. I missed her a lot.

The following week, I finally called Rauf. Apart from myself everyone in my clique was anxiously to hear the good news. The bombshell soon fell as Rauf began with "Sorry yaar (yaar meaning pal in Urdu). I have left no stone unturned trying to arrange a place for you. None of the families had any vacancy, but they too promised that they would continue to look out."

I asked Rauf if by any chance he could take me in to stay with his family. He politely explained to me that his house was already inhabited by his Abba, Amma, Bardi Amma and his four brothers. All the brothers slept on the floor spreading their mattresses apart in their singular one big room. Rauf said it was next to impossible that his Amma would agree but he would speak to his mother. "Who knows after she hears you story, she might agree."

This was the last hope. That night while tossing my head on a restless pillow, I prayed fervently with all my heart with tears rolling down my cheeks. "Oh God! You are the only One I have ever turned to and You have always found a way. So please help me now once again for You know I have never been so helpless."

The anguish I felt from this situation was leading me into indescribable state of despair for I pray no one at my then age of seventeen should ever experience. That night was the worst I was just turning side to side and finally due to deep exhaustion I fell asleep.

The next morning, Rauf called and told me that his mother had said that she could not trust "Bombay boys" because they had a bad reputation! Obviously, this was far from the truth. But she was a simpleton and so she believed what others had told her.

My heart sank and my hands began shaking in fear. I pretended I was not disappointed. Rauf then told me that his mother had invited me over for

Sunday lunch and this act of kindness softened the blow to an extent.

Embroiled within the confines of my dark and gloomy room and relentlessly bombarded with bad news, I felt like the roof was precariously and slowly caving in on me.

I felt trapped and began to realize that there was no way out. At this point, I remembered what my dad had said before the day of my departure: "Good luck. But I am sure you will come back after you will find all doors closed for you." This ostensible challenge strengthened my resolve. I was not about to give up. I convinced myself that I could handle the difficult and often sleepless nights.

I extended my after-work walks on Bunder Road from sunset to eight or nine p.m. I even began having my meals at a nice restaurant where the waiter used to wish me. By now I was a familiar face at dinner time and they had started calling me by my name: "Ali sahab, what will you have this evening?"

and so on and so forth which actually made me feel very good.

The only time when I was in that dastardly room was from nine p.m. till morning hours. I had made my bed more comfortable by spreading my own mattress on top of the hotel bed. I had got my sleep cycle back on the track in a week and slept well. The days in the office were progressing from good to one of the best times of my life for me. After all I really did have a family here who genuinely loved and helped me as much as they could.

What more did I want?

I had handled tough situations before, and this would take its due course. In my room one night I spoke aloud to my father elsewhere: "Dad, I am still here. And I am not giving up."

I was always a chatterbox, I loved to talk, and I believe this is part of my charm. It also made sense. After spending my after-work hours all by myself with nobody to talk to, in the daytime I compensated by talking perhaps way too much. When Hamid mamoo got tired of my continuous chattering- although he never got angry - he would become so fed up that he would bribe me to remain five minutes quiet offering to buy me a sweet lassi (butter milk) in return.

I felt blessed and lucky to be around these types of good people. They made my life easier and those days were one of the best which I can never forget. During daytime on the weekends it was quite bright in my room so I read newspapers which I usually picked up from the office at the end of the work day.

I was always an avid reader from my school days. At a very young age, I began with comic books which I borrowed on loan from a bookshop which belonged to one of the compound guys. He never charged for the comic books of Captain Marvel, Superman and Gabby Hayes who was best known for his several appearances in B-Westerns with John Wayne as the be whiskered, cantankerous, but ever brave comic sidekick of the cowboy stars. I had plenty of Hopalong Cassidy and Roy Rogers comic books.

As I grew older, I graduated from comic books to cowboy western books. From a very young age, I was fascinated with the American Wild West which I watched in Western movies in Bombay. I never missed a single Western release. I watched my first Western when I was eleven years old. It was

Jesse James starring Tyrone Power and Henry Fonda. I became an immediate die-hard fan of Tyrone Power and Westerns.

I loved and devoured a heap of Western books, but I especially enjoyed those written by Louis Lamour and Zane Grey. I adored their vivid writing style the most because while reading their books I could actually feel as I was riding a horse and holding on to the pommel of the saddle, heading my horse towards a russet sunset. This dream came into fruition which you may read in my third volume of my memoirs.

I also read detective novels of Scotland Yard and the crime novels of Micky Spillane which included his great signature detective character of Mike Hammer who was much later played in the TV series "The New Mike Hammer (1984) and 'Mike Hammer Private Eye' (1997) by Stacey Keach.

I asked Zaffar to buy me a Western book so I could keep busy reading on the weekends at the hotel. He said he would try and finally gifted me one which helped me pass my time. I was anxiously awaiting for Sunday for Rauf to come and take me to his home.

The long-awaited Sunday finally arrived. Rauf had promised that he would arrive around ten, and bless him he was on time and did not keep me waiting. He told me to hop in the rickshaw. I was so excited that once inside the rickshaw I embraced him. In him I had met my match in chattering. The route was very easy from my hotel, straight up Saddar Road to Rauf s house.

His home was in Bori Bazar, in a very narrow building. His home was on the second floor. The first floor was an office space. Next to the office was a tiny landing, approximately four feet square. There was a steep narrow staircase up to their home. As we approached a few cockroaches ran for cover. Rauf nonchalantly kicked them away; he was used to the bugs.

Finally entering Rauf's home, I realized that the family lived in one huge room. To the left a curtain divided the house into two spaces. Behind the curtain was a small table on which sat two stoves for cooking.

On its far side Amma and Bardi Amma slept. I now realized that this limited space was actually the reason I couldn't fit in.

I met Rauf's four brothers, the eldest being Farrok: Munna; Nasir and the youngest Muttalb. They were all friendly. However, I noticed only Farrok sizing me up trying to decide if I was a decent boy or not. The most awaited moment for lunchtime was announced by Rauf. The sofrah (long cloth) was spread on the floor, the air was filled with the delectable aroma of spicy food and my mouth was already salivating.

Muttalib spread the plates on the sofrah, while Munna, brought out the hot piping food. Rauf announced that I would be tasting their family's favourite dalcha, a yellow grounded lentil curry with pieces of meat eaten with rice. In Bombay we called it dal gosht chawal which was also my favourite. I ate like a glutton.

I had not tasted home-cooked food in ten days. I ate so fast that everyone was amused. My head was bowed down devouring the delicious meal, so I did not realize everyone was watching me in amazement. Well, I was hungry, and the food was delicious and home cooked. I was in gastronomic heaven!

According to tradition, the women of the house did not come out to meet strangers. But Rauf's mother peeked through a small opening in the curtain happily watching me engrossed in eating. I hardly noticed anything around me; I was in a food coma. After I had filled myself to the limit, I finally stopped. To top it off, I took a glass of water.

After lunch, we rested a little and then Rauf and Munna took me around the bazaar and Elphinstone Road. Unbeknownst to me then, Nosrat lived not far from there. The most important purpose for me to have gone to Karachi was to meet Nosrat. After our walk around town we came back to Rauf's home for tea.

While we were having tea, I saw through the slight curtain opening that Amma was calling Rauf. After five minutes Rauf returned with a wide a smile on his face. I thought his mother had joked with him about my voracious appetite. I thought I would be invited to lunch every Sunday which would be awesome.

However, the smile denoted something beyond my imagination. Finally, Rauf came over smiling and hugged me. I wondered what was going on until Rauf told me happily that his mother wanted me to come and live with them. I was dumbfounded it took me a few seconds to register what I had heard, and I did not believe my ears.

I asked Rauf to confirm what I had heard that I could come and stay with the family. He acquiesced and I looked up and thanked God. Then I got up to hug all the brothers one by one including Rauf again. Finally, with a loud voice I thanked Amma who peeked out smiling and shaking her head.

I asked Rauf that I was not imagining too much, but would it be possible that I could move on that very day. I received a big affirmative reply. I began to shed tears of joy while Amma was watching everything unfold. She told Rauf that I was very well-mannered and seemed to be from a good family. She said she felt safe with me in her house and further added lovingly that I was her sixth son.

Rauf and I went back to the hotel in the rickshaw to pick up my stuff; came down and settled the checking out with the manager. Rauf helped me load up. I carried my trunk while Rauf placed my bedroll under our feet, and I was happily on the way to my new family life.

On the way, to our house - yes sir, it was now my house too! - I kept on asking Rauf about the things which might make Amma uncomfortable and that I should avoid doing in the house. He told me to relax and not to worry, as it was an all-boys house and after all Amma was used to the boy's behaviour.

Rauf further added that Amma had also declared me as the sixth son.

It all felt so good and my joy knew no bounds. I felt really blessed and for the rest of the way I kept silent and thanked God over and over again.

After we arrived, Munna helped me with my luggage and placed it in a corner of the house. Amma told Rauf to explain to me that I had to pay monthly 75 rupees for boarding and lodging and to sleep in the landing one floor down.

The landing was a tiny, dark place and I had to sleep in the company of cockroaches. It was a scary thought but I convinced myself that I could live under any conditions thrown at me so I would handle this as well. By the time I settled down and got aquatinted with the brothers, it was about eight p.m. and the boys' father arrived.

That was the first time I had met him. He was a thin and totally bald man clad in a smart suit and hat Rauf introduced me to him by saying, "Daddy, this Ali from Bombay, and he will be stay with us". The father replied politely, "Ali, how are you? Welcome."

At this juncture, I realised that Rauf's father did not interfere with the household affairs which he had left completely to Amma. Dinner time arrived and once again the sofrah was spread. Daddy ate his food on a small table which he also used for typing his office and other work. He never sat on the floor with us as he was an English gentleman at heart.

We ate the same delicious dish which we had for lunch. I noticed how the plates came filled from the kitchen and placed in front of us. This meant there was no second helpings which was understandable as the family was not well off and had to be thrifty, but their hearts were full of love. The food was enough to fill our stomachs.

I was thankful indeed that I was not alone anymore; had a roof over my head and a family who loved me.

After dinner everyone sat around me asking me about my life in Bombay. I felt great being the centre of attraction and narrated In detail about my life from childhood to working in my father's restaurant and mechanical workshop and the oil refineries.

Of course, it would not be possible to narrate my whole life story in one night. Amma told us all to rest and to continue relating my incredible life journeyed next day. It was bedtime and all the boys spread their beds side by side on the floor for the night. Muttalib spread Farrok bhai's bed, someone who always came to sleep late.

It was now time for me to go down and face a lonely night with the cockroaches. It was not totally dark as the light from upstairs allowed me to see and guide myself down. I swept the place clean with a small broom that Amma had given me. I spread my bed and crawled into it. It took me about an hour to go to sleep, occasionally brushing the cockroaches off the bed.

There was only one bathroom for the nine of us which was situated about three stairs from the home space. It was a small cramped place where one could also bathe while sitting on a small stool with two pails of water which was enough to clean oneself. I knew that I would be the first one to use the bathroom so I got up very early in the morning.

I had set my small alarm clock for five thirty in the morning. I got up rolled up my bed and went straight up to the bathroom where I cleaned up, ready to start the day with my new family. I went back down to the landing, unfolded my clothes for the day which I had neatly placed under the pillow, dressed up, rolled up the bed and took it upstairs and placed it in the corner.

It was six in the morning and the boys were up, each taking turns to wash and get ready.

Amma was up before everyone, preparing breakfast which consisted of one fried egg and one chapati and a cup of tea each. I thanked God that my first home away from home provided fresh breakfast. By 7.15 a.m. I left saying Khuda Hafiz (May God be our protector) and went down to catch a tram.

Rauf had shown me the tram stop which was right opposite our street. It went straight to Bolton Market. The tram looked like an old vehicle that had seen many battles but was nevertheless safe to ride. Nothing like the beautiful trams of Bombay. It travelled at a speed of 40 miles a fortnight, taking me half an hour to reach my destination.

All in all, it was a safe trip and if I am not mistaken the fare was only two annas. So, from my salary of 125 rupees, seventy-five rupees went for room and board, and only a few rupees went for transport; the rest I could now thankfully save.

I was just in time for office and I began wishing salaams to everyone. Hamid Mamoo noticed a difference in the way I greeted everyone, saying that I appeared kind of different with a look of contentment on my face. "You look exceptionally happy," he said, I gave them all the good news about my new home and family.

They were all overjoyed about my ultimate release from the dungeon. Zaffar declared that at lunch time they wanted to know all the details. These were genuine and good folks. I never realised that individuals could be so happy about hearing about someone else's good fortune. During lunch I related the whole episode as if I was telling a fairy tale and all of them were all ears and smiles.

Hamid Mamoo declared it was my faith in God and that is what kept me going. I told him HE has always answered my prayers. I had asked Zaffar to help me buy sweets after work.

I took the box of sweets home to show my appreciation in whatever little way I could. Amma was very happy with me and said, "Beta this was not necessary." She served the sweets after dinner.

Amma always had a smile on her face, but Bardi Amma was serious but also kind-hearted. Meanwhile I had become very close to Munna. He was my age and we thought alike. Rauf was much older than us. Munna and Rauf had their own set of friends with whom they often hung out.

Meanwhile Zaffar and I became very good friends. He told me that after work, he would go home change and pick me up and we would have dinner and then go to the movies. I told Amma that I was going with Zaffar and would be having dinner with him and return home after watching a movie.

Amma told me to try and come home soon, as the family went to sleep around 10 p.m.

Zaffar finally dropped me home around midnight. I tried opening the wooden door, but it was shut. I knocked hard on the door so that the family could hear the sounds from the second floor. Munna popped his head out of the window and shook his hand with a gesture meaning he was coming down. I was relieved.

Where would I have gone if Munna had not heard the knocks, as Zaffar had already sped off. One night after dinner, Amma told me after dinner that she thought henceforth I should sleep upstairs with the boys. "It's not healthy down there," she explained kindly. I thanked her profusely and Munna told me to spread my bed next to him.

In bed we chatted till we fell asleep. After waking up and my morning prayers, I thanked God: "Thank You, my saviour. You have always tested me and saved me." I have recited my prayers regularly from the age of six, a practice that was inculcated into my mind and heart by my sweet Granny.

Days passed into weeks and weeks passed into months. At the office, I was now placed under Razak who was responsible for arranging ships once they entered into Karachi port after mooring. Once the ship was docked, Razak would go on board to meet the captain and check all the pertinent papers for customs declaration with the first mate and arrange for offloading the manifold of goods.

Razak was an aficionado of alcohol who really enjoyed drinking. The captain and the officers were aware of his weakness and habitually brought Johnny Walker and soda and placed it on the table before the checking of the cargo manifest began. Razak wanted to pour a glass of whiskey and soda for me but I told him that I didn't drink and the first and last time I had tried was a shandy.

He requested the steward to bring us a bottle of seven up and a can of beer. While I sipped my shandy he started teaching me the ropes of his job. It appeared that Razak was getting away with whatever he wanted from the ships' captain. Before we left the ship, he would request the captain for a couple of whiskey bottles and cartons of cigarettes, and the captain always complied.

On the way back, I asked him how he was commanding all this protocol and smiling he replied that the captain and the officers were very happy with his work facilitating a speedy offloading of goods. "They knew I am very good at my job and even if there was a glitch in the landing papers, I will handle it smoothly and the ship would dock and offload without a hitch."

Hassan was another of Razak's assistants. He was a former boxer, with a swarthy complexion, cauliflower ears, and a flat nose, evidence of his former boxing career. He was always smiling, revealing a gold tooth. He was a very friendly guy but unfortunately not very bright but nevertheless loved by everyone.

I told Hassan about my own boxing days in Bombay and he was happy as he now had someone he could relate to. Often in jest, he would mockingly throw a jab and a right cross, obviously missing my face and in return I would reciprocate. These special interludes really made me very happy.

At the office, everyone knew about Razak's addiction to alcohol and his consumption. But if you saw his face, you would hardly notice any sign of an alcoholic. What was amazing was he never got drunk. Funnily, either he had a tremendous tolerance for alcohol and perhaps it did not affect him as it would a normal person, or he had reached a point where he needed to drink all the time to stay sane and sober!

One day at the office, Abbas Bhai approached to tell me that he was proud of the fact that I had found myself a place to stay, something which he had not been able to do for me. "But most of all, I have heard of the progress in your work," Abbas Bhai added. He then started to tell me some upsetting news. "I have given up my activities here. Afzal will handle it all now. I am moving to Chittagong."

My heart sank and Abbas Bhai noticed the fear on my face and quickly reassured rue that he had spoken to Afzal and Wali lmam, and they had agreed to put me on their payroll. I would henceforth be an official Maritime employee. That was the last I saw Abbas Bhai and after that I always prayed for his health because he was the person who had taken a gamble on me and brought me to Karachi.

No one else would have done that for me. Afzal sahab came up to me smiling, reassuring me not to worry as the Imam family would look after me. That was a great comfort along with the much-needed assurance of my permanent job. After a couple of days, I met Shaida Imam, the eldest of the brothers and the patriarch of the family.

He was sitting in Afzal sahab's room next to Khokar sahab, whose desk was right opposite to Afzal's. A cup of tea in one hand and a cigarette in the other; he was sitting absolutely straight upright on his chair. Afzal sahab called me in to meet Shaida sahab. "This is our elder brother," he said. Shaida sahab gave rue a wide friendly smile and asked how I was. I instantly took a great liking to him.

Now that I was well-established in the offices of Maritime Agency, I related to Hamid mamoo the sad story about my great true love Nosrat and I. He listened with great interest and patience, finally declaring that it, indeed, was sad. I told him I had to find her telephone number by hook or by crook and speak to her just once, come what may.

Hamid mamoo, now established as my confidant, advised we that although the whole episode was sad I had to learn to forget Nosrat and move on.

But I insisted I had to speak to her just once and then that would be the end of it. He acquiesced and asked me where he should begin. I told him I thought Nosrat's husband owned either gas stations or a construction company, but I did not know his name.

The only lead I could give was that he had married a Persian girl from Bombay. After a week, Hamid Mamoo's friends called and gave him a telephone number, hoping that it was the correct one, and if not, the matter would be closed. I anxiously dialled the number with great apprehension. A lady's voice on the other end said 'hello' and I quickly realized that it was not Nosrat.

After wishing her salaam I asked if I could speak with Nosrat. In my heart I was praying to God that it was the right number.

I realized my heart was thumping so loud and if it did a little more it would burst, and I would collapse. The lady asked who I was which meant that this was indeed Nosrat's house number. I replied quite calmly that I was a friend of Nosrat's brother from Bombay and he had asked me to call her. She said Nosrat was taking a bath and to please call back after an hour.

Those sixty minutes seemed like a whole day

Hamid Mamoo realized that it was the correct number, and I thankfully replied "Yes. Thank God!" I excitedly dialled again exactly an hour later. Nosrat picked up the phone. It was so nice and almost surreal hearing her voice. "It's me, Alladin," I said, full of hope. In her mild voice - she was always sweet, kind, gentle, and soft-spoken, and for that, I loved her even more. She replied graciously. "Alladin, how are you? How is your mum?" Nosrat knew my mum also still loved her.

I told Nosrat that this is the first and last time I would be calling her just to ask one important question: "Why in God's name did you agree to this marriage?" I remind her of our last picnic date on Juhu Beach, where during the gentle flow and ebb of the tide, we both swore that we would marry each other no matter what. I kept on talking incessantly, prolonging the conversation as long as I could because I knew this was the last time, I would be talking to her. "Your sister Ezzat had already warned us, of your mother's intentions to get you married in Karachi. But what happened to our oath?" I asked.

Nosrat replied in a sad voice, "I know all of that and I am sorry. But I just couldn't win against my mum. I was helpless." That was the last time I ever spoke to the first true love of my life. I was sad during the rest of the day. Hamid Mamoo and Zaffar tried to console me by telling me that it was over, and I should not hurt myself any further over something which I had no control. Hamid Mamoo quickly ordered my favourite lassi to take my wind away from the sad situation and I was ready to move on.

As time went by, Zaffar and I were becoming extremely close and considered each other as best friends. This bond was a great source of happiness for me. Imagine being best friends with Zaffar, the youngest brother of the Imams, who were owners of the company I was employed at!

This put me right on top of the world. I missed all of nay family but especially my sister, Meher, and my little brother Farrokh the most. Each of them regularly wrote to me at least once a week, keeping me abreast of our family's goings-on.

Nokoo was out of Meher's life; married and gone, but there were many in the compound who would have loved to make Meher their wife. One of these ostensible suitors was Hadi, Mehdi's brother (vol 1). However, Hadi never approached Meher as he was a shy boy. But he would visit my father regularly with the hope of glimpsing Meher. If he had mustered up enough courage and asked her hand in marriage, my father would have agreed, because he was handsome and a good boy from a very respectable family. It was a shame I was not there otherwise I would have encouraged him to talk to my father.

Then there was Sadru, my boxer friend, who was secretly in love with Meher. One could not mistake that look on his face whenever he saw her. As much as I loved Sadru, that was not a possible union. Farrokh always wanted to follow in my footsteps, so he took interest in school dramas, and like me always landed the lead role. He kept me informed about his plays and his progress with his school studies. Farrokh had developed an intellectual mind from a very tender age.

After dinner, Munna and I always took a stroll around Elphinstone street. He introduced me to Mohsen, the owner of a bakery and a very pleasant guy whom the gang called 'the king', probably because he gave them free cookies and cake. Munna also introduced me to a Catholic girl called Thelma who was a bit of a plain Jane especially with her glasses who was also thin and taller than me.

One day, we were at her house and she exclaimed that the coming Sunday there would begin a series of jam sessions replete with snacks and cold drinks. Thelma asked me if I danced. "Hell yes!" I declared. Then I began to relate to them about our Bombay jam sessions, where we danced nonstop from eleven in the morning till five in the afternoon. When we were hungry, we had sandwich in one hand, and just continued to dance.

Being young, we had a lot of energy. After watching Bill Haley and his Comet's first film 'Rock Around The Clock' - which was all rock and roll, and epitomised the dance of the 50s - over and over again, I had become a great rock and roller. I remember the film first premiered in Strand cinema in Bombay where the kids went wild dancing to Haley's tune, right in the cinema house. Later the tunes became an ubiquitous mainstay at all dance halls.

The film had not yet come to Karachi, arriving couple of months later. Thelma thought it was great that I was an experienced dance freak. "Ali can you teach me? I already jive so it will be easy for me to learn", Thelma begged. I spent two hours teaching her the steps and how to partner with me because it was not easy to follow my steps and to keep up with me because I was too fast on my feet. Usually, kids took one step on a beat, but two steps on a beat as I did was pretty speedy and difficult.

On the day of the jam session, Munna and I put on our smartest attire to impress the girls. This would, after all, be the first time I would be among girls since I had arrived in Karachi. There was a small entrance fee as the organizers had to rent the hall for the session. Then there was the income from selling snacks and drinks. If they made some money, or even if they broke even they would continue the event regularly.

We were among the first to arrive, after which a huge crowd thronged. We all sat on chairs which were neatly arranged around the hall. I looked around to see if there were any pretty girls. I was kind of disappointed, because none of them met my standards of being pretty, let alone beautiful. The emcee took to the microphone and welcomed us.

"We hope you kids will have a great time. Enjoy your food and drinks, but above all we are here to dance, so dance your troubles away and rock till you fall. So, without any further ado, let's start with the opening number, Bill Haley's 'One Two Three O'Clock Rock'" This particular song by Bill Haley actually made rock and roll popular and famous in the 50s and beyond. It had taken the world by storm.

The music and the beats thundered throughout the hall and we all began dancing and showing off our steps. After one dance, I sat down and told Thelma to continue dancing with other partner as I wanted to observe the others dance and discern which of the girls was a good dancer, so I could try with her. I was disappointed to see that none of the dancers were really good and a far cry from Bombay's dancing girls and boys.

Each couple was trying hard to do its best, but as if they were going out of their way to attempt some steps which did not jive well with the beats.

Then right in the centre of the dance hall I noticed a couple. The boy was short, about five feet and two inches, while his partner was about five feet four inches. They were both very dark complexioned; she had short hair and was pretty. She wore striking read lipstick and I said to myself I wouldn't mind having a girlfriend like her.

I noticed the couple could not rock and roll, but they danced the jive so well that I loved watching them dance around with such ease and smooth steps. It looked as if they had been dancing together for a while. I wish she was my partner, for

Thelma was too tall and clumsy. This girl would learn fast and it would be easy to do the dancing acrobats with. I as Jed Thelma about and she told me the boy's name was Shaft, while the name of the girl now escapes me.

"They are number one dancers in Karachi and whenever there is a friendly contest they always win," Thelma explained. Rightfully so. But the new champ has come to town and their reign has come to end I mused to myself. In the film 'Rock Around The Clock', there is a dance sequence, which symbolized fad of Rock and Roll. During the dance, the dancer announced, "While I'm dancing man, don't talk to me I'm on the seventh cloud."

They were high without consuming alcohol. The creative dance steps were beautiful to watch and not everyone could perform them. The thundering rhythmic beats of the band shook movie halls and dance halls. Imagine if in those days they had the surrounding sound systems! I've always described the rock and roll dance actually went through one's body, straight to one's feet and made one instinctively swing whether one knew how to dance or not.

I had never attended dance school nor had I a dance teacher ever. I had innate rhythm and had learnt my dance steps by watching 'Rock Around The Clock' over and over again, all the while it played In the cinema house. Before the movie, we used to dance in parties the slow Foxtrot at Christmas balls, New Years, and on terraces where the tenants of the building held these events regularly. Recently, 65 years later I watched the movie over ten times on the Turner Classic Movie channel in the USA. I had mastered each and every step except the split which I could never do. In Bombay I was considered one of the best dancers although there were many couples who were damn good.

At Maritime, I related my Sunday dancing escapade and Hamid Mamoo smilingly said that he did not know that I was also a dancer. Zaffar was very interested and asked me if he could join us the next time. I replied in affirmative. Zaffar had never been to such an event before. The jam session had made money for the sponsors, and they had announced that it would be a weekly event.

The following Sunday, Zaffar picked us up from Munna's house and drove us to the event. As we stepped in Zaffar's eyes were trying to take it all in, and I could see he was very excited.

He did not know how to dance, not even the slow Foxtrot, but he was just content to be in the dance hall. Meanwhile I had taught Thelma a few new steps and how to also hold my hand while I did the back bend and other moves.

'Rock Around The Clock' broke all movie records. The headlines in American entertainment papers read, "Bill Haley is a Big-Wiz". The parents of the crazed kids were enraged, labelling the movie's choreography as "The Devil's Dance". They held town meetings all over in America to ban this kind of evil being spread in their society. Some towns buckled under pressure and ultimately had to ban it. But not a pack of wild horses could stop the kids. Dancing was arranged in the outskirts of towns and kids piled up in packed jalopies - what convertibles were called at that time - to reach their destination.

No one could stop the spread of this wildfire which was the precursor for all who came after like Little Richard; Chuck Berry; Jerry Lee Lewis and finally the King, Elvis Presley. The following Sunday, Zaffar came to our house and we went to the jam session together where a huge crowd had already assembled. The kids now had one more place to go out and enjoy. One could see their excited and happy faces ready to go and let off steam.

The dance began. I tried some new steps with Thelma, and she did well. We had performed some new steps which the kids had seen for the first time. I saw that Shafi was also watching me with interest and a little jealousy. After all, he had always been the centre of attention. Every weekday in the evening at Thelma's house, our gang got together dancing and Thelma learning new steps. Moshen always brought cookies and cake. After a lot of pain and practice Thelma and I were talk of the town.

On weekdays, going to work at the offices of Maritime Agency with all my favourite people was the norm. One day Wali Imam sahab called me for the first time in his cabin. Looking directly at me, he told me that henceforth he wanted me to do some work for him. I replied, "I would be happy to", as I was garnering an opportunity to please him. He explained to me the intricacies of his warehouse where he wanted me to go and take the inventory of the stock; check how many bales there were, while being mindful not to miss any as they were all stacked one on top of the other.

Wajid was instructed to give me enough money to cover my rickshaw and lunch expenses because it was going to be a full day's job. I completed the task by three in the afternoon and returned to the office. Wali Imam sahab was surprised to see me back so soon. As I was handing the list over to him, he asked me if I was sure I had compiled the complete inventory. I assured him I had and not to worry as I was a fast worker. He was very pleased and from time to time I continued to handle this task.

After work, Zaffar and I went out practically every evening. He sometimes took me to the movies and to a nightclub, called Le Gourmet in the Palace Hotel. He would sign the bills which went directly to Afzal Imam's account. Afzal sahab was a regular at the club; popular and loved by everybody, especially the waiters as he was a generous tipper.

Going out every night meant, coming home late. Amma had told me nicely not to stay out late. So one night I asked Zaffar to take me home early, explaining the situation which was causing problems. It was also becoming inconvenient for Munna to keep on opening the door for me. Zaffar suggested that I could stay with him the nights we were late as he had one quite large room to himself with an extra bed right opposite to his. I asked him if his Bardi Bhaby or Shaida Bhaiya may object and he reassured me that they wouldn't.

As usual I got up early in the morning, and while I was praying, Bardi Bhaby entered to wake up Zaffar who was responsible for driving her kids to school after breakfast. Bardi Bhaby was a beauty with movie star looks.

With great difficulty, Zaffar woke up and introduced me to Bhaby in his sleepy voice. "Hello. So, you are the boy that Zaffar has been talking about," she said very sweetly with her large hazel-coloured eyes looking at me kindly.

After breakfast, we dropped the kids to their school. Zaffar then told me their names. The elder child was a girl called Shakila, who I think was about eleven, and her younger brother Shakil was nine. Shakil had beautiful nearly blond curly hair and Shakila had a milk white complexion and golden locks. By the grace of God, they were both beautiful children.

By now the kids at the jam sessions had all improved in their moves which made it possible to try other dance partners. The emcee took to the mike and announced to us kids that he had great news for us. "We have rented a bin hall for the next jam session," he announced enthusiastically. Before he could finish his sentence, the kids went wild with excitement. The emcee who was spontaneously funny then said, "ladies and gentlemen please behave like ladies and gentleman!" Again, the kids went crazier.

He went on "We are going to hold a dance championship. and the winner will be awarded a cup", he concluded. This time the screaming and shouting was so loud that it literally shook the room. Needless to mention, the loudest were the girls.

We had one week to prepare, and I did my best to teach Thelma, but she was taller than me and not very flexible. I wish I had someone my height and flexible and dexterity who was also a fast learner. Then I would have shown the kids what Rock and Roll dance really is. But I had to manage with whom I had.

The much-awaited day arrived, and all the hopefuls came with anxiety written all over their faces. There were a lot of new faces who came for this event I had not seen in the jam sessions. Shah of course was there with his regular dance partner. I began sizing up the floor, preparing for the opening steps for the finals which would be something new and also not from the inspirational rock and roll film. I was sure Shafi and I would be competing with one another in the finals.

The rented dance hall was located on the premises of a grammar school. All the contestants were on the floor with their respective dance partners, waiting for the music to begin. After the emcee announced, "Good luck," The first dance commenced. Four impartial judges were chosen to walk around the throng of dancers and eliminate couples, who were not up to the mark. After the first round six couples had already been cast out and they humbly joined the spectators who sat on raised benches and watched the rest of the dance with them.

It took about ten dances till almost all the other couples had been eliminated, except (as I had predicted) Shafi and I and our respective partners. Confident that we were going to be in the finals, I had already explained to Thelma about our final entry. The emcee announced Shafi's and my name for the finals. The music began and Shafi started his jiving which he was good at but rock and roll was different animal altogether! One jived but with faster beats and acrobatics.

Al eyes were on me, but I did not start right away. While Thelma was standing at one end, I walked to the other end. The crowd was puzzled. As soon as I reached the other end of the long hall, I shouted "Go!" Then Thelma, and I started dancing towards one another on one foot and then slide forward with the other feet tapping to the beat backward and forward moving in sync till we met right in the center of the floor.

As soon as we met I picked her up and swung her around my back and as soon as she landed I started rocking and spinning her very fast left to right while I, with my knees bent was doing a very fast two steps to a beat. No one else could accomplish this type of choreography as it was very difficult. It took me a sleepless night to plan this and prepare for the dance.

The audience roared and we received a standing ovation while the music continued with Thelma doing her best to keep up, especially after that rocking and spinning her made her a little bit giddy. But it was enough the music finally stopped, and everyone anxiously awaited the name of the champion couple to be announced. Ten judges counted their votes nine out of ten judges picked me as the new champion.

Zaffar and Munna, along with our gang, were the happiest and they all came down on the floor congratulating us. Zaffar and Munna hugged me and even Shafi and his partner came and congratulated me. I told Shafi, "You two are smooth dancers your jiving is great." They were all smiles.

The jam session continued till 5 p.m. By then, lots of girls rushed towards me wanting to reserve a dance with me. Yes, I had arrived and was here to stay! I was on cloud eleven and basking in the effulgence of my glowing success. 1 think I handled it with as much humility an excited and jubilant seventeen-year-old could muster.

Boys and girls came up to me introducing themselves. One of them was a guy shorter than me who introduced himself as Abbas Namazee. He told me he was also Iranian and from Bombay like me. I was very happy to meet him and our friendship lasted a long time, flourishing even more when we in Teheran together which will be expounded upon in Volume Three.

A second young gentleman to approach me was a Kuwaiti Arab living in Karachi named Mustafa Elmarzook. "I would like to be your friend and would like to invite you for an evening out" he said politely. He was tall and slim had a thin mustache, wore glasses and had a very friendly smile. I accepted his invitation but told him that I usually go out with Zaffar and Munna and asked if they could come along. "Oh yes sure! The more the merrier!" he declared happily.

Mustafa took us to the Metropole Hotel, which had a nice restaurant. While we were enjoying our meals and drinks, Mustafa told us how he had arrived in Karachi with his older brother, Jasem, and their mother. The family was in the import and export business, importing quality Medjool dates and exporting textiles among other things.

Mustafa, whose nickname was Musti, became a very dependable and good friend whom I could count on. He would do anything for us and from day one I knew I could trust him. He was about three years older than me and same age as Zaffar.

I was still staying with Munna and his family. In the evenings, we continued with our regular walks on Elphinstone Street. During our walk about six friends joined us. I was the leader of the clique as they all looked up to me because I was both very popular with the girls and I was also known as the "King of Rock 'n' Roll", a name I was referred as reverentially at dance halls.

Our clique's popular hangout spot was at an Iranian restaurant where we enjoyed tea and snacks including bun maska (the latter an Indo-Pak word for butter) and other treats. Our next stop was Thelma's home where we reached in time for the hit parade of Rock 'n' Roll songs on the radio. This medley included the songs of Bill Haley, Little Richard, Chuck Berry and others.

One of the latest was a rockabilly song first recorded in 1956 by Gene Vincent called "Bee-Bop-a-Lula." We all really loved Gene and the energizing song catapulted him right on the charts for weeks.

Meanwhile Zaffar, Musti and I were out most evenings. Both of them smoked, so when they offered me a cigarette, I told them that I don't smoke but I will try all the same. The first drag involved me coughing so hard I felt my eyeballs would pop out.

Then I decided to just blow the smoke out without ever inhaling. I had also started drinking beer, which I must confess I had begun to enjoy a lot.

Saturday evening outings meant late nights, with the result that I was becoming a regular and overnight guest at Zaffar's house. On Sunday mornings, everyone woke up late for breakfast. One Sunday when we were all seated at the table when I heard Shaida sahab calling me to his room in a kind of a stem voice. I froze in my shoes. I looked to Bhaby with the hope of support because the command sounded ominous. She just smiled at me reassuringly.

I stepped cautiously into Shaida sahab's room and after saying salaam stood respectfully at the furthest distance as possible. He told me that he noticed that I was sleeping at his home practically every night. At that moment my heart nearly stopped, I thought that now the guillotine is about to fall, and he will tell me kindly not to come to his home anymore. He smiled and said "Go right now with Zaffar and bring all of your luggage and belongings to stay here. We are adopting you as our son." He said kindly.

I was shocked. Did I hear right? I tried desperately to express my joy and attitude, but words would not come forth. All I felt were tears rolling down my cheeks amid my wide smile. Shaida sahb knew I was extremely happy and thankful, so he told me smiling to enjoy finishing my breakfast.

Zaffar was extremely happy to hear about this new development. Now he was reassured that we could come and go as we pleased. After breakfast we took the old model Bedford van to Munna's house and on the way Zaffar told me that he would teach me to drive. This was great news because 1 always wanted to drive and was anxious to learn. I assured Zaffar that I would be a fast learner.

Once at Munna's home to pick up my belongings, I first went to Amma to tell her the news. She was genuinely happy for me. I kissed her hand and moved it to my forehead as a gesture of deep gratitude. I told Amma she had been a real mother to me and that I would never forget her and whenever I craved dalch, (lentil curry with meat) I would not hesitate to visit.

All the brothers surrounded and embraced me. When I was hugging Rauf, I told him as a real brother that he had made this all possible for me, offering me my first home and family away from that god forsaken dungeon. "Ali, yaar it was a pleasure" Rauf replied sweetly. As Munna helped me with my luggage and I was leaving, Amma and Bardi Amma said with a smile "Ali my son remember this will always be your home. You are welcome here any time, and we will make your favourite dalcha whenever you want."

We were soon on the way back to my new home, a spacious bungalow situated in P.E.C.H.S., a quiet and peaceful residential area compared to Bori Bazaar where I had previously lived. The bungalow had a large eagle figure on its rooftop as a landmark so that visitors could easily find the house. One just had to say "Cheel wala Bangla" meaning the eagle bungalow.

While Zaffar was driving us home, I was silent for a moment. I closed my eyes and thanked God over and over again. "YOU have helped me from a young age from all difficult and impossible situations. I acknowledge before THEE all the blessings YOU have bestowed on me." Gratitude towards HIM was taught to me by my grandma from a very tender age and I have never forgotten this invaluable lesson. I asked Zaffar to stop at a sweetmeat shop where I picked up large box of the best sweets to take home.

Everyone received and accompanied me to our room where Bhaby had placed a small table by my bedside. I shoved way luggage under the bed whose bed sheets and pillow felt so fresh!

Between Mazhar sahab's room and ours, there was a large bathroom which also included a toilet. I could now enjoy bathing luxuriously!

After lunch, Zaffar took me for driving lessons, after he had asked Shaida sahab if the van was available. We set out to a deserted place not too far away from our home where my driving lessons officially began. After the initial jerks, bounces and releasing the clutch too soon, I was on my way to becoming a driver. To Zaffar's great surprise, by the third day I was able to drive around the area surrounding our house.

On the fourth day Zaffar announced that we were going to drive to Bori Bazaar but warned me that I had to be alert there as it was a crowded locality. Once in the car we headed towards Bori Bazaar. It was easy sailing till we entered the heavy traffic area. At this juncture Zaffar began his instructions in a soft voice so as to not to get me nervous, which I already was. I now knew I had to stop talking and with nay undivided attention just drive.

Zaffar was a real darling and very considerate. He knew if he spoke a little loudly, I would make error. By the grace of God, I made it to Munna's house after circling twice around the block to park on the street closc to his home. We went in and fetched Munna and all three of us went for a drive, stopping for refreshments on the way.

Munna could not believe that I was driving "Arey Ali when did you learn to drive?" Munna asked with an incredulous expression. "Ali learned to drive only in five days," Zaffar replied proudly. "What? So Soon? That's unbelievable!" Munna exclaimed. After a little while we headed home.

The day after I had moved into Zaffar's house, Wali Imam sahab and Afzal sahab, both got to know of the move. They each called me to their rooms and welcomed me into the family with big smiles. Hamid Mamoo was also really very happy; it was written all over his face. He told me that I really deserved all this happiness.

Once back home, Shaida sahab told me to henceforth call him "bhaiya" (brother), like others did. He continued: Wali Imam is Sanday bhaiya Afzal is Afzalia and then there is Mazhar bhaiya. Of course, in the office to maintain their respect and decorum you must continue using sahab after their names. I felt I was really at home. I was provided food, a nice roof over my head and it was all free of cost!

I tapped into my savings which I had begun from Munna's house, and I asked the tailor who worked right under our house in a small tailoring shop to make a few items for me. This tailor could make anything even jackets. I had him make me a warm, coarse wool jacket and a kurta pyjama set. Now that I could save even more, I later got made two sports shirts and a couple of pants to match.

Bhaiya was a writer; he used to write throughout the night, drinking tea and chain smoking right up to around four in the morning then go to sleep. We had three drivers among us. Zaffar and I alternated in driving the kids to school which was not too far from our house. When it was Zaffar's turn, he most of the time rolled in his bed and in his sleepy voice would ask me to take the kids to school. This was fine with me as I was an early riser.

After my prayers I happily took Shakil and Shakila to school after their breakfast.

There was also an official driver who was on duty from eight in the morning to five in the afternoon. After we had our breakfast, he drove Mazhar Bhai, Zaffar and me to the office and returned to the house; completed some household driving chores for Bhaby till Bhaiya woke up whence he then took him to office.

Bhaiya really lived like a nawab, having his breakfast around eleven which often consisted of his favourite, basen ki roti and very hot mango achar. He polished off at least two cups of tea in the morning, before he set out for the office where he continued drinking tea throughout the day with snacks.

Bhaiya had written some books in Urdu language which he had mastered. He was now busy writing a film story and trying to finish the film script.

Although he had not told me at that time, but he had written a role for me after he had come to know from Zaffar about my rock and roll talents and my Bombay screen test.

Completely oblivious that my life was about to change, I continued working and learned as much as I could about shipping as I could. I had learned a lot while simultaneously handling Sanlay Bhaiya's warehouse. All the Imam brothers were very pleased with my work ethics.

Sometimes Musti would insist on coming over in the evening after work to plan a night out. I always took permission from Bhaiya and he being very easy-going individual encouraged me to go out and have fun. Zaffar often joined us but sometimes he was tired and then I would go alone with Musti.

These excursions ordinarily meant late nights so I would go to Mustis' to stay overnight. He introduced me to his mother, a very kind lady who spoke very little Urdu, but understood other's speech. Musti loved her to death and would do anything for her. He would change his car each year for an upgrade and he loved his Ford. When he drove the new car out of the dealership he would go straight home and make his mother sit in the passenger seat and take her for a spin. This was his way of attaining blessings for his new car.

During the days when I had walked with Munna and the gang on Elphinstone Street a complaint had been sent to the Iranian Embassy about us. They complained the gang was led by Ali an Iranian. We had not done anything except the boys sometimes passed harmless remarks to girls passing by.

As I was Iranian, and I had entered the country on my Iranian passport I had made some friends at the Embassy including Javed who was the secretary to the Ambassador of Chamber of Commerce. Saved had lived a long time in Karachi and was fluent in both Urdu and English. He called me at Maritime offices and told me that I had better visit his office soon.

He did not explain the reason on the phone, and I got a little worried. 1 took permission from Afzalia and went to Javed's office. Once there, he told rue that the police had complained that I had been seen to behave like an aimless vagrant on the streets of Karachi with the gang. I explained to him exactly what we did, and he told me not to worry anymore. He then said the other reason I called you is that the Ambassador of Chamber of Commerce wants to meet you.

Javed took rue to the Ambassador's office and introduced me. He was a tall, very fair handsome gentleman. We conversed in Persian and he told me in a very friendly way not to forget that I was Iranian and that I should not have behaved in such a disorderly manner, "Javed has taken care of the problem" he told me solemnly. To my surprise he added: "By the way I want to request you to teach my three girls Rock 'n' Roll dancing."

His daughters had Pakistani girl friends who belonged to the higher echelon of society and attended the same school. I was really surprised that they had heard about me. Replying to his request about my teaching the girls I said in Persian: "Rohe cheshrnam qurban" (on my eyes sir). Then he offered to pay me to which I replied "Qurban khejalt nadeen" (please don't embarrass me) I will not accept any money it will be an honour to teach them.

Out of the three sisters, the eldest - I think her name was Soraya - was much more striking looking than her younger sisters who were girl-next-door-types. I told Soraya I would teach them "the reserved way." Incredulously she asked me whatever did I mean. I explained to her that I would teach them to be good dancers but without the acrobatics, because to indulge in that aspect would be unbecoming for the daughters of the Ambassador.

Laughingly, she told me not to worry as her father was liberal in this respect. I was relieved. To my surprise, Soraya and the youngest learned part of acrobatics while the middle sister mastered only the basic jive. In between practicing we took breaks during which I spent time reading Iranian magazines eating fruits, pistachios and sipping Iranian tea. My eyes widened as I saw beautiful girls dressed in modern Parisian-like dresses amid fancy cars. I silently muttered to myself: "I must now visit my own country."

By now, I had become proficient in teaching my friends how to dance. One Sunday Zaffar told me that he would love to learn to dance because he had never danced in his entire life. I told him that I would be pleased to teach him gladly, but it would begin with slow dancing only, like the foxtrot, and a little bit of jive because I knew my brother Zaffar was a square!

After breakfast, I gave Zaffar his first lesson to slow music by Benny Goodman. I took part of the girl and told him to look down and watch my steps and to just follow. It took him over an hour just to learn the basics and another hour for me to teach him how to gently turn his partner around. Eventually he began dancing, leading me without looking down. He was a little stiff, but I was sure he will learn to relax.

We took a break, had some tea until it was time to learn to jive, again to the music of Goodman. Teaching Zaffar to jive seemed almost an impossible task. If it was anyone else, I would have told them to forget it and just dance to the slow numbers. But this was Zaffar whom I loved a lot.

I sat on the floor and took Zaffar's feet in my hands. I told him to relax them so I could lift them up, and tap them on the floor, rhythmically in each beat, alternating his left with his right foot. This went on for quite a while and was really about to give up, my back and hands were paining, but he eventually kind of got it. After lunch we had final tutorial of the day.

While we were resting, I told him to close his eyes and imagine he was in a dance hall. Once the music commenced, he should begin tapping the floor with his feet; get into the flow, slowly shake his head rhythmically and he would eventually learn to dance.

I continued to remind Zaffar to stand upright, close his eyes, listen to the music, and let it flow through his body right up to his feet. "I promise you will dance with confidence. Confidence is the key to the whole thing and pretend there's no one on the floor except you and your partner." I encouraged him. Zaffar then asked me who taught me to dance. I told him no one had taught me but that I had been born with rhythm and was later inspired by watching the film series on rock and roll.

One Saturday I spent the night at Musti's house and the following morning after breakfast he asked me to accompany him to check his goods which had arrived at the warehouse. Apart from owning a car he also had a scooter on which we rode, with me on the backseat.

As we were approaching the docks, I experienced a flashback of how I had arrived here just months earlier. Once again, I witnessed the similar scene of a camel cart stopping right next to the traffic police with the camel's head precariously hovering over the traffic policeman's turban. He was not alarmed because he was used to this interaction. I on the other hand was what would happen, God forbid, if the camel did not stop and trampled the policeman.

At around two p.m. we headed back to our house after Musti had checked, all the gunny bales full of Medjool dates. At the traffic crossroad waiting for the policeman's signal, a motor rickshaw stopped right beside us. The passenger recognized Musti and after greeting him told him that Susie had been involved in an accident while shooting for a film and was now admitted to a hospital.

In a concerned voice Musti asked his friend Eddie when the accident had occurred, and Eddie replied a couple of hours earlier at Hawk's Bay Beach while shooting for a film scene. She had been standing on a rock waiting for the director to give the cue. When the director shouted "Action" Susie slipped and fell on the sharp-edged rocks.

Musti told Eddie to go ahead and we would follow him. Turning his head towards me he introduced me to Eddie. "By the way this is Ali." "Ali Reza the King of Rock 'n' Roll?" Eddie asked incredulously. I smiled at Eddie while Musti acquiesced. Eddie seemed to be in awe, and with a wide smile said he was very happy to meet me. While we were following Eddie, Musti commented that by now the whole of Karachi probably knew about me as some local Urdu film and entertainment newspaper had also written about me.

We arrived at the hospital and it looked like a typical film scene with everyone there: the heroine in the hospital bed and the director and the cameraman by her bedside making sure that their heroine was okay. After the film crew bid farewell, Susie's mother, sisters, Eddie, and Musti approached her bedside. I was standing far away talking in Persian with one of our Embassy guy who, I later found out, loved Debora Susie's older sister. She didn't care for him.

Also standing was a bespectacled lady with a very kind face. I was observing the whole scene from the end of the room thinking to myself what all this fuss was about. All the while hcr family was fussing around her, Susie was watching me. She finally asked who the boy was standing in the back. Before anybody could turn around to see me, Eddie proclaimed: "Oh Susie you won't believe it but that is the King of Rock 'n' Roll Ali Reza."

She called out to me "Ali please come and sit beside me on the bed." Her family was kind of puzzled and was wondering whether I was famous or something. I could see in Susie's eyes that she fancied me. "Yes, I have heard about you Ali," she said. "I hope one day you will teach me and we will get to dance together which will be a great honour."

A heroine saying all of this to me was somewhat overwhelming. I told her we would see, shook her hands and told Musti that we should now leave. Susie seemed taken aback and Eddie pleaded for us to stay a little bit longer. Musti agreed and began to introduce me first to Susie's mother to whom I respectfully nodded my head and said, "A pleasure" and then to Sarah Aunty. Without any hesitation I embraced her and exclaimed "Very, very pleased to meet you," I don't know what overcame me, but I was automatically drawn towards this very kind lady whom I had been observing from the moment I had entered the hospital.

Sarah Aunty embraced me back tightly and whispered in my ears that from now on I was her son. The rest of the group was taken aback wondering what had drawn this boy to Sarah Aunty without me ever having met before. But she emitted such motherly love which filled my heart with love. I later learned that she was not married and was childless. Before leaving I also met Deborah and Baby the youngest sister, whence Susie invited Musti to her house as he had not been there in a while and please bring Ali with you.

I always eagerly awaited letters from my sister, Meher, and brother Farrokh. My mum missed me a lot and kept on telling my siblings to ask me when I was returning to Bombay. I used to lovingly laugh at my mother's insistence as it had only been a few months since I had left Bombay. But a mother's love knows no bounds.

My brother, Saifu was by now disinterested in attending school and one day told our father: "Baba don't waste your money any more, I'm failing in school and it would be better if I come and help you in the restaurant."

Without hesitation my father accepted the proposition gladly and soon Saifu was taking care of the Cold Drink House full-time.

I wrote to my sister Meher about my good fortune of living in a bungalow with Bhaiya whose youngest brother, Zaffar was my best friend and like a brother. In my letters I mentioned that I knew our mother had consistently been praying for me and my good fortune was the fruits of her prayers.

I wrote to them about everything and everybody in my life. It is not often that everyone who was once in a desperate situation like me when I first arrived here, in just a few months living in comfort with loving people. I was truly blessed, and I still thank God every day after each prayer. My younger brother Farrokh in one letter wrote that he was becoming popular in school just like me. His first girlfriend was Nargis whose house was next to ours. I remember she was very pretty and petite like Farrokh. I was very happy for him.

Mazhar sahab had developed a great fondness for me. He would habitually take me aside, and if he noticed something which required his guidance and expertise, he would advise me like a father would. One day he told that henceforth he wanted me to call him Mazhar Abba, meaning father.

Again, for the second time my eyes were moist with gratitude and love. From then on, he was my Mazhar Abba.

Even Bhaiya had gotten used to me calling Mazhar Abba. Often while talking to me he would refer to his younger brother as "your Mazhar Abba." I was so happy and yet afraid at the same time lest I lose all of this love with a single unintentional mistake. But then I would reassure myself that they all loved me so much and would never be disappointed but instead forgive me and guide me.

Afzalia was preparing for his trip to Japan to meet ship-owners like Mitsubishi et all as 99 per cent of the ships Maritime handled were from Japan. These trips transpired at least once every six or seven months. On his return he would bring everything whatever they had requested before his departure and believe you me the list would often be a long one. I did not ask anything it was not my place to request something for myself. If he had asked, I would have requested a single silk shirt. But for now, it was merely a dream. Perhaps on his next trip, Afzalia might also ask me what I wanted from Japan.

Bhaiya noticed that I was neatly dressed to the office daily with well-ironed matching trousers and shirts, even though I had to circulate four pairs.

Every night Bhaiya would ask Bhaby to place his own trousers and bush shirt for the day on the ironing board so that the Pathan boy who worked for us night and day would iron Bhaiya's clothes accordingly.

In the morning the boy would serve bedside tea to all of us, placing cup next to our beds and simultaneously call our names to wake us up. This was a novel and momentous experience of being pampered. No one had ever served rue tea in bed before nor had such comfort ever come my way. I began feeling like a "chote nawab" (young royal). I felt elated and after I received my first bedside tea, I asked Zaffar if this routine would continue every morning and he said this was a regular custom in homes that could afford it.

One evening after our movie night, Zaffar told me that he was taking me to a small tea shop where he had not been in a while. He forewarned me that the ambience might disappoint vie but told rue that the tea is one of the best. Zaffar drove right up to the shop and parked in front of it. A boy came out and Zaffar ordered two kardak chai with extra malai (strong tea with extra fresh cream). I had never enjoyed such delicious tea in Karachi.

Sitting in the car we had just finished our tea, and as the boy was collecting the cups and saucers, we heard the thundering sound of horse hooves beating hard against the ground so hard we thought an earthquake was taking root. As I looked out from my side glass window to check what the commotion was about, I saw a frightened horse coming straight at me with the carriage driver trying to stop him but to no avail.

Raising his front two legs the spooked horse came straight down on my glass window, shattering it to pieces with splinters flying all over. My immediate reflex forced me to duck my head, right up into my lap. Had I not ducked my face would have been ruined. Zaffar also ducked but we were really very badly shaken.

The driver got down and kept on apologizing while trying to calm down his horse by striking him gently talking to him. He then took the horse and carriage away walking with the horse. Zaffar checked to see if I was alright and I did the same but by some miracle we were both unscathed. Zaffar sighed and told me he couldn't believe how we had both escaped injury especially me.

"If you had been one second late in ducking, you would have lost your good looks," Zaffar said. I replied that God loved us. To calm our nerves Zaffar ordered another two cups of tea which really calmed us. As we were leaving, I felt my thigh becoming wet. When I checked the palm of my hand it became wet with blood. I rolled my trousers up to my thighs and saw a small piece of glass lodged in my thigh. The bleeding continued to flow and Zaffar told me to press hard on the wound after I had removed the shard of glass. He then drove me straight to the hospital. The nurse bandaged me up and soon released me. After over 60 years, I still bear the scar.

Sanlay Bhaiya suddenly became ill and was burning with a temperature of 104 degrees. He lived in Clifton, one of Karachi's posher areas, was unmarried and lived alone. Zaffar and I brought a doctor to his house who gave Sanlay Bhaiya a shot and medicine to be taken ever six hours. A Pathan boy worked for him night and day but Sanlay Bhaiya couldn't depend on him. He told Zaffar to drive the doctor back and Sanlay Bhaiya told him that I would stay with him.

I checked Sanlay Bhaiya's dressing table to see if he had a bottle of 4711 Eau De Cologne but was disappointed. 1 wanted to use the same method my granny had used on me to reduce my fever since I was six years old. In the absence of cologne, 1 just used strips of cloth soaked in cold water and placed them on his forehead replacing it with another as soon as the cloth became warm.

I did this for two hours till the fever had dropped to 102 degrees. We were still not out of the woods. Around eight p.ni. Bhaiya, Bhaby Afzalia and Zakiya Bhaby came to visit. They brought with them two big bowls, of chicken soup and toast. Zaffar had brought my kurta pyjama, and toothbrush. They asked Sanlay Bhaiya how he was feeling, and he replied that he had to thank me, who had helped reduce his fever by two points and he was sure I would not rest till he had completely recovered.

The Pathan house-help warmed up the soup, placed it in a bowl with spoon and brought it on a tray and Bhaby fed Sanlay Bhaiya. Zaffar and I sat in the dining room where I ate curry and rice because I was really famished. At around ten p.m. they all left. I kept on with my treatment, giving Sanlay Bhaiya his medicine on time. I gave him two aspirins, which he initially refused until I convinced him that the healing method, I had been using thus far was my granny's and that he should trust me.

He finally took the tablets and I covered him up well with an extra sheet and I told him he would sweat profusely. After about 45 minutes Sanlay Bhaiya cried out that he was drenched in sweat and to please help him change. I asked the house-help to bring a clean kurta pyjama and a towel and he helped me pick Sanlay Bhaiya and sit him upright.

I dried him with the towel and helped him out on his kurta while he changed his pyjama himself and slept like a baby.

In the morning, Sanlay Bhaiya woke up and called out to me while I was saying my prayers in the guest room. As soon as I finished, I rushed to him and he looked at me and smiled.

He told me he was hungry, and I felt relieved. I checked his temperature and told him that it had returned to normal at 97.6 by the grace of Allah. I told the house keep to give him hot tea toast a little butter and honey and nothing else. 4"he entire Imam clan came to check Sanlay Bhaiya's health and were surprised to find him sitting in his drawing room dressed in his robe sipping tea.

I went home with Bhaby and Zaffar to change into fresh clothes. On the way Bhaby told me that she was really proud of how I really took care of Sanlay Bhaiya like a nurse. I told her that I did what my granny used to do for us when we fell sick. Later Zaffar dropped me back to Sanlay Bhaiya's house because he wanted me to stay one extra night as he had not yet gained all his strength back. That night I slept in the comfort of the guest room like a baby till morning and so did Sanlay Bhaiya.

We enjoyed a hearty breakfast with two fried eggs and toast for me, and one boiled egg and toast with honey for Sanlay Bhaiya. After breakfast we sat in the living room and he asked me to recount my story from Bombay to then in Karachi. "You see how busy I am in the office, so I have never got to know much about you. Now that we have time, please tell me your story," Sanlay Bhaiya asked politely.

I smiled and told him that my life thus far could fill one fat big volume, but I would try and give him the gist of it. After he heard, that from age of six I had been working and after all I recounted he was very touched and told me that I was a real fighter, and he was sure that I would fulfil my destiny and find my place in the world.

That evening, the whole family came to Sanlay Bhai's house who had ordered premiere cuisine from a top-notch restaurant in Clifton. We all enjoyed the tasty food specially me as I always had a voracious appetite. After dinner while we were having tea, Sanlay Bhai told the family that he wanted them to know that without my care he could not have recovered so soon. "Ali really nursed me back to health, staying up the whole night and I'm very thankful to him", Sanlay Bhai glowed thankfully. I could see on Shaida Bhaiya's face a smile of pride. I felt great and replied that I was always happy to help the family.

Within the premises of the Maritime office Wali Imam was extremely strict with everyone; even Zaffar and Mazhar Abba. Woe betide for anybody who made a major work error as they would be summoned to his office and given an earful. Zaffar and Mazhar Abba both smoked, but ncvcr in presence of Bhaiya or Sanlay Bhai. Afzalia however smoked in front of everyone except Bhaiya and Sanlay bhai.

The respect the brothers held for each other, was rare and something I had never seen anywhere. It was wonderful to watch the younger brothers speak so gently and with utmost respect to their elders. I had never witnessed any of them speaking in a loud voice, even if they did not agree on something.

One day, Zaffar had apparently made a major work mistake. He was called into Wali Imam's office, realizing he had mixed up some documents. In his hurried fear Zaffar had forgotten to leave the cigarette in the ashtray before going in. In the office Afzalia was standing behind Sanlay Bhai and when he happened to see the cigarette, in Zaffar's hands, he stepped back and made repeated signs with his fingers to alert Zaffar to exit and throw the damn cigarette away.

It took a few seconds for Zaffar to realize his stupidity during which time Sanlay Bhai glared at Zaffar's fingers. Zaffar dashed out of the office;

extinguished the cigarette and darted back in to face the problem and was merely told to be more careful. This ls just one example how the brothers showed respect for one another. After Zaffar returned to his seat he asked Hamid Mamoo, for another smoke which helped reinvigorate him and calm his nerves.

I forgot to mention that when Afzalia returned from Japan he brought a beautiful sport silk shirt and a pant piece for me. I was so happy that he thought of me. Children always called him "Acche Abba "(nice daddy) and rightfully so. He was indeed very acche and loved by everyone.

At least once a month either Afzalia or Sanlay Bhai invited the whole family to dinner. That meant great variety of delicious food. Zakia Bhaby Afzalia's begum made sure the cook prepared all the dishes just as she had directed.

Reminiscing about Zakia Bhaby, one's first impression of her might be that she was a very serious and snobby person, but when you got to know her she was really a very friendly and considerate human being. However, she had a penchant and reputation for driving her latest Chevrolet model car extremely fast like a maniac. But as far as I remember she was never involved in a serious accident.

Sometimes she asked me to accompany her when she went shopping. When I accompanied her while she drove, I used to pull myself straight up in the seat, with my feet, pressing the ground. She was high strung and did whatever she wanted. not caring for anybody's opinion. She was a free bird, soaring high above everyone but she loved her family with all her heart. At that time she had three children, Sabrina, Godoo (Azam) and Tootu (Amjad) who was the naughtiest kid.

Zakia Bhaby ensured that her table was always filled with different dishes and her cook was really good. Sanlay Bhai's dinner parties were equally good covered by a Bihari cook who I believe also worked for Haleem Sahb, former Vice Chancellor of the prestigious Aligarh University. The food at both places was absolutely delicious, but my favourite, was the Bihari kabab at Sanlay Bhai's which I could never get enough of. While I am writing this my mouth is literally salivating at the memory.

We would often all venture to a hut at Hawke's Bay Beach, an expansive and beautiful seaside locale. 1 don't remember if Afzalia owned it or rented it each visit. We would ride camels and have camel-back races.

Shakila and Shakil would ride together as did other kids.

I had become quite good at camel-riding and was capable of making the camel go pretty fast which was fun. We took a picnic lunch from home of really tasty snacks and hot tea in flasks. We either relaxed in the sun or in the shade, whatever our preference. It was one of the best days.

Afzalia had an extra car, a second-hand Jaguar which Zaffar often drove with Afzalia's permission. We used to take some of the girls who, I had introduced Zaffar to in our jam sessions to the beach. He was very shy when I first took him to a dance after he had learned to dance. But he would not go to a girl asking for a dance. One day I walked Zaffar towards a girl and told her to dance with him slowly and to be extremely patient with him. That is how he gradually gained confidence with each dance.

On one such occasion as we were returning from the beach, Sanlay Bhai saw us, he was very strict and did not approve of our behaviour. He was angry at Afzalia for allowing us to be so free with girls. When Afzalia met us the next day he informed us that unluckily Sanlay Bhai had seen us with the girls. I then had to listen to a long lecture full of advice. "For Gods' sake be careful!" Afzalia implored. Now you know why we all call him "Acche".

Afzalia was a regular at the nightclub 'Le Gourmet', visiting at least twice a week. Sometimes he took Zaffar and myself and it was okay for us to drink alcohol in his presence. He was cool, laid-back and not strict like Sanlay Bhai. He told us to remember to be very careful and ensure that Sanlay Bhai never got a whiff (literally) of any of this.

Eventually Zaffar was allowed to sign on Afzalia's account, and we used to go to the club alone. We also took some friends, including Musti and Razi, a great still photographer. An Anglo-Indian boy named George, who we had befriended from jam sessions also sometimes joined us.

For the main attraction 'Le Gourmet' always had the best foreign artists contracted for at least a month and if they were very popular then the contract would be extended. On one such occasion they had hired a well-known dancer from Hawaii, who came with her own band. She was a knock-out with a voluptuous, near perfect figure. Her name was something liked Hawaii de Lolo.

The first night of the engagement Afzalia never missed and he took us along with him to the club. It seemed that he had already met Lolo before, and he had her twirling around his finger. With what we witnessed; I can safely conclude that they were having an affair. We were sitting at Afzalia's table and when the main attraction was announced, and the moment Lolo stepped on the floor everyone was awestruck.

The Hua Pahu - tall drums started to beat with the other instruments in perfect sync which in confluence was pleasing to the ear. Lolo began her dance with her hips shaking to the beat of the drums and her hands portraying a call to her lover. In comparison the Tahitian dance had faster drumbeats and involved faster hip-swaying movements.

Halfway through her performance my dance impulses took over me, and before I knew it, I had grabbed a dinner knife in one hand; jumped up and then falling to the ground on both knees, slid in a bent sitting position all the way to Lolo. I stopped right next to her and while sitting down on the ground, I lifted the knife pointed towards her to take it and stab me. The crowd all rose to their feet clapping and in loud voices encouraging me to dance with her. I got up, threw the knife on the floor and did my best to follow her motions. Afzalia was very pleased with me and laughing embraced me. Zaffar, too, was very happy.

One Sunday morning Musti came to pick me up from my new home for a drive. Everyone from the Imam clan was already familiar with him. After cups of tea we went for a spin. On the way, lie informed me that we were going to Susie's house. "What! Count me out just take me home," I implored. "Let's not spoil our Sunday" I added. Musti pleaded with me to change my mind because he had promised Susie that he was coming. "Please be a sport and come with me for my sake" I finally gave in.

When Musti knocked on the door, Susie opened it. Surprised that this was the same girl I had seen in the hospital. In all fairness, she had undergone a trauma but her smudged make-up and mascara all over her eyes made her look unattractive when she was in fact very pretty. I noticed that her long and silky hair grew right up to her lower back. I'm a sucker for long hair.

Smiling she thanked me for coming and ushered us in. "Musti, my dear, it's been a hell of a long time," she told her childhood friend. We sat down in the family's small living room. An excited Eddie was the first family member to enter, then the rest of Susie's family joined us.

I met Susie's daddy for the first time. He was tall, had a crew-cut and was blind. He extended his hand to welcome me and Musti. Then my dear Sarah

Aunty arrived. I jumped up and embraced her because she had accepted me as her son at our first meeting. Everyone noticed that we had developed a bond which was somewhat extraordinary. Musti and I left after a couple of hours, promising that we would return to visit.

Susie's family lived on the first floor of a one-floor building situated in Gandhi Gardens. An Iranian Bahai family lived on the ground floor. In those days not every house had a telephone as it was costly to install and the monthly charges were equally expensive. Whenever Susie or her family wanted to make a call, they would go down to their neighbours and call from there.

Susie called Musti and invited us to Sunday night dinner. Musti called me and told me to keep that night free. I requested him to ask Susie if I could bring Zaffar along. Susie told Musti that Zaffar was most welcome. Zaffar was excited to be meeting a movie star. After Zaffar met all he sat next to Deborah and started talking to her.

Once we were seated at the dinner table Susie made sure that I was seated next to her. Her family had prepared chicken curry and rice which was quite tasty. The curry was filled right to the top in a large bowl and everyone served themselves after elders had taken their share. When it was my turn, Susie stood up and personally served me with a larger portion than others.

I was visibly embarrassed because everyone had their eyes on Susie. After dinner Susie put on rock and roll music and asked me to teach her to dance. I asked her that in spite of working In films why had she not learnt how to dance. She replied of course she knew how to dance but wanted to learn rock and roll steps. I had taught Zaffar and Musti how to dance and now this girl wanted to learn. I was kind of getting fed up with teaching.

Musti cut in and announced it was time to go for a car ride. We all somehow managed to fit in the car with Susie ending up sitting on my lap. We went to Clifton beach; walked on the sand enjoyed ice cream and Musti made sure that he paid, after all he was quite rich. After a little while we returned to Susie's home. Musti was simply the best, he was genuine and would do anything for a friend.

Going to Susie's home, having dinner, and then venturing to Clifton Beach had become a weekly affair for us. Sometimes Musti would tell Susie's mum not to cook as he would bring Bondo's chicken, naan, and kuchumber (mixed salad). In those days Bondo's was famous and people from all over came to eat there. Since my childhood I had a weak stomach. If I was not careful with my diet, I would develop cramps, and often times diarrhea. It was no different in Karachi.

Whenever I would get such attacks, I would lie on my stomach face down on Eddie's bed. My darling Sarah Aunty would always come and sit next to me and gently caress my hair to comfort me. The she would give me a dose of some white liquid which always helped. Eddie considered me as his brother and loved me a lot and his feelings were reciprocated.

Susie's family were interested to know about my family and nay life in Bombay although Susie herself had cousins living in Bandar, Bombay. They were all amazed by my long and difficult journey from the age of six to the then present time. I had become proficient at retelling my story using lot of sensory details. Susie's family were completely absorbed as if they were experiencing the events while I was reminiscing them.

All the details I narrated, as God is my witness, were factual and not fictional stories. Susie's mum was most impressed and touched as it is usually mothers who deeply feel children's pain and joy. She also loved me genuinely like her son and addressed me thus. Now, if that's not a blessing from God, then what is?

Musti, Susie, Eddie and Deborah had attended the same prestigious grammar school and so had been great friends for a long time. It was clear to me that Susie was Musti's girlfriend and there was no reason to think otherwise; it was a given. The way they behaved so close laughing and enjoying one another's company. But what I could not comprehend at the time was that whenever we were with Susie, she would always try to endear herself to me.

For example, she would go out of her way, to serve me more pieces of meat or extra chicken legs. Even when we had ice cream, she would give me an extra scoop than to others. I was tiring of these awkward situations and to avoid them, I told Susie in a soft voice not to serve me so much as my tummy could not take it. "Please let me serve myself as I know my stomach better than you. Okay?"

I pretended not to notice the disappointment on her face. She was genuinely hurt but tried to hide it behind her smile and I also felt for her. I kept on getting stomach cramps, especially if the tasty food I loved came from the restaurant. There is a saying in Farsi, "Ager kharbozeh bekhori pahe larzesh bayed benshini" (if you eat honeydew - usually harvested in winter - you will shiver with cold) alluding to after effect of eating melon in the winter season.

I was lying on Eddie's bed on my stomach, face buried in the pillow with cramps, I thought I felt Sarah Aunty, sitting next to me on bed as usual to comfort me. 1 told her that I would be alright and to just give me the white syrup. The caressing continued, but I did not hear her usual consoling words that I would be fine.

In my daze I heard Susie saying it was her and not Sarah Aunty, I jumped up in the bed, my pain suddenly evaporated. "Susie what are you doing? Please go away before anyone sees this, especially Musti! I can never allow this! He is my best friend and brother please go away!" I implored.

Susie tried to hug me, her eyes full of love "Ali believe me, Musti is not my boyfriend," Susie insisted "He never was. He has always been a great friend since our school days and he still is just that," she added. I pushed her away, telling her to stop all this emotional stuff and jumped out of the bed and rushed to the bathroom. I returned fresh-faced as if nothing had happened and joined the others. Sarah Aunty asked if I was feeling better and I said yes.

Sarah Aunty had observed Susie and was sure that Susie loved me very much. Later she told me in a motherly manner that Susie really loved me and had never felt like this way for anyone before. I told Sarah Aunty to forget this whole episode and that I did not want to get involved with Susie at the expense of losing my best friend.

That night, we didn't go for a spin to the beach but instead sat down and played cards. It was getting late, after kissing mum and Sarah Aunty, Musti and I left. It was late so I went to Musti's house to spend the night. I needed a drink so Musti pulled a hidden bottle and we each had a couple of glasses and then went to sleep.

In the morning I had a mild headache and debated with myself whether I should share last night's episode with Musti. I hesitated thinking I might break his heart. But while having tea in bed, I told Musti that I needed to get something off of my chest and tell him what all had transpired the previous night.

I told him to please listen to the whole story before rushing to any judgment. I related every moment while 1 had been on Eddie's bed and how I had told Susie not to try and hug me or talk about being in love with me because she was your girlfriend and I would never in my life betray you.

After patiently listening to me, Musti in a series tone told me that I had done the appropriate thing and that I had definitely proven that I was not only his best friend but also his brother. I told Musti that I was relieved and that I should no longer go with him to Susie's house. It was then that he burst out laughing. I looked at him in puzzlement, Musti then explained in a brotherly manner that Susie was never his girlfriend but just a great friend.

Her manner of demonstrating friendship was just so personal that people often got the wrong idea. "She is a damn good girl," Musti encouraged. "My advice to you is go for her. She is the best thing that will happen to you. She will love you fiercely with all her heart. This I can promise. What I am worried about you is that you are a bastard and she will endure many sad days."

"Knowing Susie, she will not stop trying till she wins you" Musti added. The thought of it all excited me. Susie was a good-looking girl and she loved me with all her heart. This was evident from the way she had tried to embrace me with tears in her eyes. As I put it altogether, I finally convinced my heart and decided that I would tell her that she could be my gal but no mention of love in the beginning.

Meanwhile Susie telephoned Musti after a couple of days that she had fallen in love with me the very first time she saw me in the hospital. She said she knew that it sounded corny, but it was true that she had never felt like this before. Musti reassured Susie and told her that he had clarified with me, that she was his best friend. Period.

Musti further added that I had made no commitment. "Let me warn you Ali is a big flirt and you will have sad days" Musti warned Susie. She replied that she will take her chances and told Musti to please bring me to her house. Musti a real good friend to all, was going out of his way to help Susie.

He related to me in detail their telephone conversation and begged me to go to her house with him. I told Musti, I really didn't know what was the rush and that we could go next week as we usually did. In most girl's opinion, I was considered somewhat conceited, but I never fed their pride by showering them with praises in the hope that they could become mine. I ignored them till they came to me themselves.

In retrospect I believe losing my first true love Nosrat due to her mother's scheming, made me kind of conceited. The anger associated with losing her, was the main reason behind my somewhat callous behaviour towards girls. Now Susie would be the first poor girl who would experience heartaches by falling for me.

Musti called Susie and told her that I was finally coming over. When we knocked at the door, Susie appeared and Musti entered with me following cautiously behind. Susie looked at rue with hope and I encouragingly winked at her and she got the message with a big Smile on her face.

This was the beginning of a long affair, a mash-up of love, tenderness and heartaches, the latter always caused by me. Susie had begun to call me in the office, and since I was sitting next to Hamid Mamoo, I told her to always ask for him, and he would pass the call on to inc.

Once Susie came to Muhammadi House where Maritime Agency was located, to meet her elder sister Deborah who also worked in the same building. So, one day Hamid Mamoo, Zaffar, Susie, Deborah and I met downstairs at the restaurant for lunch. We sat on the corner table and I introduced Hamid Mamoo to Susie. And oh boy they became very close to one another right away! Zaffar and Deborah were busy talking to one another.

The reasons being that Hamid Mamoo was soft-spoken, kind and loving and furthermore Susie was very easy-going, very friendly, and never flaunted her heroine status. Hamid Mamoo knew what sort of a bum I was with girls and he told Susie that if I ever troubled her in any way to call him and he would take care of me. In jest Susie shook her hand at me and said now that she had Mamoo on her side I should be careful henceforth.

Zaffar, Musti, Eddie and I were spending more time with one another. Musti never maintained a steady relation with any one girl but instead with many and they were all casual. Eddie on the other hand was desperately in love with an Arab girl named Farideh who lived close to Eddie's house.

Farideh's family was very strict so she often had to sneak out to meet Eddie.

Zaffar had developed a liking for Deborah but was too shy to approach her. I tried my best to guide him and made sure he got to spend alone time with her. But instead of romance he would speak to her about the Imam family. Even on picnics In Hawks Bay he used to be alone with her on the beach he never broke the ice. He could never open up to her in spite of my teaching him how to.

Unlike, Susie Deborah was extremely reserved, and I didn't blame Zaffar entirely for not being able to break the ice with her. I even told her Zaffar was interested in her, but she only displayed a reserved smile with no comments. She had great character and poise. There was a guy in her office whose name was also Zaffar. We called him motoo (meaning fat) and he was always going out of his way to do favours for Deborah but to no avail as she similarly never encouraged him.

Then there was Deboo Bhatacharyya, a Bengali music director, with hit songs to his credit. Very rarely did a Pakistani song became hit in India, but one of his qawwali song did. He used to coach Deborah with her singing as she was a regular radio singer. Deboo loved Deborah immensely with his whole being, and her alone. He was a jealous hot-blooded man who could hook up with any girl from the film industry if he wanted to, but he never even gave them a second glance.

I was with Susie, and Deboo was crazy about her sister. Deboo and I became very close, like brothers. One day I was at Deboo's place and he took a sharp knife, held it over the fire and told me to offer my forearm. When I did, he made a big cut on it. Then he cut his own arm. We placed our bleeding wounds together and henceforth became 'blood brothers I still have the scar after 60 odd years.

Deborah had a soft corner in her heart reserved for Deboo, and she too loved him and would not show it or at least that's what I thought. Deboo later confirmed my doubts. Whenever Deboo met me the central topic of conversation was always Deborah. He knew he would have to stay a bachelor all his life as he didn't see a chance of attaining her and he just couldn't love or even like another girl.

Life went on. We worked hard during the day and in the evenings, once or twice a week we entertained ourselves in a nightclub, with movies or other excursions. Zaffar and I usually reached home after midnight and Lasha Khan, the night watchman was always there to meet us and let us in.

Every night, Zaffar and I used to open the fridge quietly and gobble all the meat chunks from the curry, leaving only the gravy in the bowl. Each morning Bardi Bhaby used to scold us reminding that Bhaiya also enjoyed meat curry for breakfast apart from his favourite hot mango pickle and bread. She used to complain to Bhaiya that we "two devils" had eaten up all the meat the previous night. Bhaiya remained cool, just smiled and jokingly asked us whom had we left the curry for? We could only put our heads down, in shame.

One night, when we came home late as usual, Bhaiya called me to his room. When I was at the door of his room, he told me to come in and sit." I now want to tell you something, which I had kept from you" Bhaiya began with a glint in his eyes. "I have completed the script of our movie, and I have added two scenes for you.

In one you will be facing the famous Indo-Pak Charlie Chaplin, and in the second there is a rock and roll dance. I know you will be able to handle the dance flawlessly but will you be able to face Charlie Chaplin?" Bhaiya concluded with a questioning look. I told Bhai that I had always been cast in the lead role in all my school plays as well as having experience directing some plays. I then related how at a very tender age of around 12, I had ventured to the Bombay Film Studios, and without any introduction approached the Director Jagdish Sethi for role in his film. He arranged for my head shots and voice tests. I passed.

"No one can intimidate me Bhaiya. I will not let you down," I told Bhaiya. "You have a good resume beta (son), but Charlie is a different creature. But don't worry just before shooting I will guide you." Bhaiya replied. It was past midnight and I went to bed. Zaffar was fast asleep but I wish he had been awake as I was desperately dying to share this good news with him. I began speaking to God, for HE always listens. "Thank you, Lord,"

I did not sleep till morning when the house help brought us tea in bed just as Zaffar was waking up. I immediately told him of the great news and the long discussion with Bhaiya. He was happy for me.

"Knowing you Ali, I am sure you will do great," Zaffar said encouragingly.

After dropping off the kids to school, I returned for breakfast. "Abhi hamara beta actor bangaya" (Now my son has become an actor) Bhaby glowed. I was already feeling like a star. Mazhar Abba was also excited for me. A new chapter in my life was about to unfold.

That morning in office, Bhaiya, Afzalia and Sanlay Bhai were in deep discussion about the film. Nobody was allowed to disturb them except for the doorman who brought them tea and lunch. The meeting went on till evening when Hamid Mamoo declared that he had never seen the brothers engrossed in such a lengthy meeting. I told Hamid Mamoo about the film and my role in the film he was very pleased and happy.

Eventually the driver dropped Mazhar Abba, Zaffar and me home except Bhaiya. We waited anxiously for him to return home. Bhaiya arrived home around dinner time freshening up after a shower joined us for dinner. He was quite whilst eating and mulling to himself, while we were dying to hear about the film meeting.

After dinner we usually had tea. During this time Bhaiya finally started laying out and disclosing the plans. A separate company was to be registered by the name of Movie Makers Ltd headed by Bhaiya as The Managing Director. The other two brothers (Wali and Afzal Imam) would be the company's Directors. Sanlay Bhai would obviously be the comptroller, as he did not trust his brothers with finances as Afzalia was a spendthrift while artistic Bhaiya had no knowledge of finances.

Mazhar Abba would be the Production Manager while I would be his assistant. Mazhar Abba and I would henceforth be the employees of Movie Makers, I wanted to let out a whooping yelp but I momentarily restrained my feelings of joy until we were done with our meeting and then I went out and let out a loud whoopee. Bhaiya saw me from the window shook his head in amusement and smiled.

Till the official registration of the film company, we would continue to be Maritime employees and then be transferred to Movie Makers Ltd. it was all in-house anyhow because the owners of Movie Makers Ltd were the same as Maritime Agency. Hamid Mamoo was equally excited and told me that I had received what I had always wanted my whole life but that he would still always be there for me, which was reassuring.

By now, Bhaiya had already decided who he needed to assemble for the film crew. He invited the director; the technical controller; the music director and other key players. The director of Photography (DOP) the cameraman and assistants would soon follow but for now this was merely a skeleton crew.

It took well over a month of meetings; going to the studio; renting an office in the studio making sure it was fully equipped precisely with all furniture and stationery used in a film production office before things got rolling.

Bhaiya told Mazhar Abba and me that this office is not like other offices where you worked 9 to 5, here you might be two three days without going home.

The other Imam brothers were not involved in this process as Bhaiya was taking care of it all in meeting after meeting. Each of the selected crew would then sit with Sanlay Bhai to come to terms. Mazhar Abba and I were not involved in all this either, except that we both visited the studio office and got familiar with the manager of the studios and others. But we were anxious at the same time to get involved especially me as my dream was now becoming a reality.

I sat down to write a long, detailed letter to Meher my sister in Bombay without leaving any minute fact. I wrote about the time Bhaiya first told me about the film till the present time. I wrote to her that I would let her know when production actually began. Meher told my dad all these details and she wrote back that he had a big smile on his face and had exclaimed: in Farsi "The son of a gun finally got his wish to act!" My mum like most emotional mothers smiled while shaking her head side to side, with tears flowing. Oh, how I loved her!

I could not wait to tell Susie about my film-acting debut as she was already an established actress. My visits to her home had become more frequent. On Friday nights her family would have Shabbat dinner to which I was always invited, and I would sing hymns in Hebrew with them. Shabbat dinners always included kosher chicken curry and rice. After dinner and relaxed I would pretend to go the washroom and Susie would follow. It was there that we experienced our first kiss; the smooching becoming like an after-dinner desert for me. I told Susie's family about the movie, and that the muharat (premier ceremony) would take place in a month's time. They received the news with great joy with my Sarah Aunty being the happiest.

We continued to go dancing and when on one occasion when the rock and roll music began Zaffar still had not jived because he lacked confidence.

Susie had accompanied us to the dance, so I instructed her to dance with Zaffar. Told her to start with patience and soon Zaffar was dancing, first very stiff but after Susie helped him to relax, he danced well. I still laugh when I think that even Zaffar had asked Susie to build up the tempo gradually.

I was always tempted "to go all the way" with girls, while necking and kissing but as mentioned earlier, I didn't want to ruin any girl's reputation, so I always controlled myself. Susie like me also had a high libido and when two lustful teenagers come together the there was a possibility of "you know what."

Susie and Musti were becoming regulars at Imam house dinners as we had all developed a fondness for them. Susie who was blessed with a loving nature and it was difficult not to like her. When Susie telephoned our house, Bhaiya usually answered phone and he would call me by teasingly telling me that my "girlfriend" is on the phone and I should come and get it. This would embarrass Susie to no end.

One-night Zaffar and I went to bed early for a change and were soon fast sleep until Bhaby came in to wake us up. It looked like something urgent had come up as Afzalia was on the phone and wanted to talk to us both. "Oh God I hope, he is not in trouble", I thought to myself. Afzalia spoke to Zaffar for a few minutes and hung up.

Zaffar told me to hurry and get dressed as we had to get to the docks immediately and he would explain the issue to me on the way. While we were driving fast, he explained that one of Maritime ships was mooring out at sea, and a young deck-boy on board was seriously ill. The captain of the ship had radioed into the port authorities who in turn had called Afzalia.

The boy had a ruptured appendix and if not transferred to a hospital, he would die. Zaffar drove as fast as possible and we soon arrived at the port. We contacted the official there who gave Zaffar some directions. I could not make head or tail of what the official had said and Zaffar said he hoped he had understood the directions properly otherwise we would only be lurking circuitously in murky, unknown waters.

It was a dark night and to our bad luck there was no moonlight. The best mode of transport we could acquire was a small motor launch. Zaffar gave its driver the general directions and we were on the way. The driver kick- started the motor which sounded ancient with an odd "phat phat" sound. I was never so scared in my entire life as I was then. I told Zaffar that we are going to drown. Zaffar told me not to be scared and silly and explained that these drivers navigated the motor launches night and day; that we were in safe hands and not to worry.

There were many ships moored out at sea waiting their turn to enter the sea-port because when the port was filled other ships had to moor out at sea. The port official had warned Zaffar that there would be many ships, but that when we were about to approach the Maritime ship we should start swinging the light on the motor-launch and the ship would reciprocate once they noticed our light.

These instructions had been relayed directly from the ship's captain and were conveyed to us. The launch's small oil lamp was a far cry from bright guiding light, and I was worried that the ship would not be able to discern it. Fifteen minutes went by and half of my life with it. But thankfully (Ahh! A sigh of relief) the ship finally noticed us and soon began waving its light in our direction.

We sailed alongside the ship and the captain appeared on the highest tier of the deck, so much so that we had to bend our heads backwards to see him. From right up there, he thanked us in Japanese accent for coming and said they would lower the patient. "Please make sure the launch is steady," the captain implored. Gradually the ill boy was lowered while the driver held both sides of the launch with his hands to keep it steady.

Meanwhile Zaffar and I held on to the boy, gently laid him down and after waving goodbye to the captain sailed away. We finally arrived at the wharf. The driver helped us to carry the ill sailor and gently place him in the back of the van where there was ample place. I sat on the floor besides his stretched-out body while Zaffar drove. I could discern from the sailor's face that he was in agony as the pain had been so intense during his prolonged time on the ship.

God only knows how long he had suffered in pain till we reached him. He kept pressing his hands to the side of his stomach where the excruciating pain was stabbing him. I tried to comfort him with words. "Don't worry, you will be alright. We are nearing the hospital." I told him. The poor soul did not understand a word of English, but he knew I was comforting him and offering hope which was the only thing I could do.

Zaffar drove straight to the Seventh Adventist Hospital, a ride which took us about thirty minutes but felt like twenty hours. Afzalia was influential and had already arranged for a surgeon who was waiting for us. The surgeon had instructed the nurse at the desk to rush the patient to the operating theatre without asking for us to fill out any forms as time was of the essence because ruptured appendixes if left unattended could cause death.

The surgeon rushed out as soon as the nurse paged him and met us, while the patient was being rushed to the operation theatre. We asked the doctor the length of time of the procedure and he instructed us to return home and rest as it would be a long night. "Besides I can see you guys have gone through a harrowing night," the doctor said with genuine concern." Return in the morning and God willing we will have a healthy patient," he added encouragingly.

We welcomed the suggestion and gladly went home. Afzalia was waiting for our phone call. As soon as we reached home Zaffar called and informed him of the ordeal and he was very pleased to hear about our efficiency.

Bhaiya as usual was awake busy writing and he usually went to sleep at around four in the morning. We threw ourselves on our beds and before you could say Jack Robinson, we were fast asleep. No one woke us to take children to school and they were happy to get an unforeseen holiday.

Bhaby suggested to let us sleep as we had earned it. We got up around noon; took a shower had brunch and rushed to the hospital. Afzalia was already there in the doctor's office and we were ushered in. When we knocked and entered the doctor's office, he got up and greeted us with a big grin, "You young men saved the life of this sailor," he glowed. Through a Japanese interpreter the recovering sailor had told the doctor that he was eager to meet us and thank us. Afzalia - our Acche Bhaiya- embraced us and told both that we had made him proud and he knew he could always count on us. The appreciation felt very good.

Zaffar and I went to see "our patient". He smiled widely with his lips extending from one ear to the other. The interpreter sat next to him. Although he had undeniable lifesaving surgery he attempted to get up and greet us bowing his head in a typically polite Japanese fashion and repeated: "Domo arigato gozaimasu" meaning "Thank you very much." We at least knew that much Japanese as we had met many principals from the Japanese shipping companies. Afzalia could actually converse in Japanese much more.

The young boy did not realize that he had been holding on to our hands tightly until the interpreter told him politely to let go, which he did with a big smile. We left the hospital and went straight to the office where Sanlay Bhai called us into his cabin. "You both did a great service to our Agency," Sanlay Bhai glowed. "The captain who was informed through the radio that the sailor was saved wired to his principals in Tokyo."

The principals in turn had called the Maritime Agency office and thanked Sanlay Bhai in the absence of Afzalia who was the main liaison between the two organizations. Hamid Mamoo, Mazhar Abba (Khokar sahb, for the first time) all gathered around and kept praising us. We were feeling like heroes. Khokar sahb opined that none could have done what we two had achieved. In the end my boxer friend threw a boxing move and hugged me and Zaffar. All the accolades were very heart-warming.

Every morning after the boy served us tea in bed, he would iron Bhaiya's pant and bush shirt. But when Bhaiya saw how neatly my creaseless clothes were ironed he instructed me that henceforth I would be responsible for ironing his clothes as I did a better job.

Bhaiya visited a murshid (spiritual guide) every Friday night as he was an ardent believer. The place was a long way from our home, and we had to traverse through the cemetery as a short cut. I would always drive him there and when we arrive Bhaiya sat down in prayer and guidance with the murshid. I sat way in the back and prayed.

The meeting used to last a couple of hours and frankly I used to get bored. After midnight we took the same route for home driving through the burial grounds, in pitch darkness with only the van's headlights on. It was an eerie experience to say the least. I believed in spirits unlike my father who never believed in them. This is an opportune time to share my dad's experience.

My father also had to cross through burial grounds in Sirjan Iran with his donkey. He was around 15 years-old and people often warned him from taking that route during the night. But he did not believe in spirits and travelled through the cemetery all the same. One night when it was a full moon and one could see afar quite a distance; my father saw a lady calling him from afar with continuous motion of her hand.

My brave and young father decided to check the apparent apparition for himself. He led his donkey, on which there was a load of flour and as he came closer, he saw a torn, long piece of cloth blowing in the wind and no woman in sight. He told the villagers of his experience and suggested not to spread stories of ghosts.

On the other hand, I once witnessed an evil spirit take over one of our friends in our compound in Bombay. His name was Ismail, and everyone called him Baboo. He was so thin and a weakling that we often joked that if a slight strong wind would blow, he would be carried away with it. One night it was past midnight he urinated under a Peepul tree and the evil spirit took over his body.

He returned home his eyes fiery red with growling voice and started flinging things about in the house and when his father tried to hold him down to calm him, Baboo just swung his hand and his father, who was a very strong man literally went flying, across the room. With all the commotion neighbours rushed to help. We witnessed a few strong adults having a difficult time holding Baboo down but eventually managed to tie him up.

Baboo continued to growl with his mouth wide open which was a scary sight. You could see this was not Baboo this was the devil. A Muslim priest who performed exorcism was called next morning. He sat on a chair and asked all of us to place a tied-up Baboo between his knees. The priest pressed his index fingers in each of Baboo's ears and after saying a few minutes of silent prayers asked the spirit his name.

"Rajarao", the spirit in the thin body, growled. The priest went on to ask the spirit what would it take for it to leave the boy's body. "Place two chickens under the Peepul tree where Baboo had actually urinated after midnight" the spirit growled. Baboo's father ran bought two chickens and as soon as he placed it under the tree the spirit left. Baboo slumped with his head down and the priest eased him down and untied him. "He is alright" the priest declared. Baboo slept the whole day and night and by the following morning he did not even remember the drama. Kids will be kids so from then on we teasingly called him Rajarao.

Back to Bhaiya and me, on our way passing through the burial grounds and us getting a flat tire. "Christopher Columbus! How am I supposed to change the tire in darkness?" I screamed inside my head. Fortunately, there was a small flashlight in the dashboard. While Bhaiya kept the light on the wheel, I managed to change it with great difficulty. I was so relieved. Bhaiya still in a tranquil mood kept silent all the way home. He was always quiet and at peace on our journeys home after his soul-connecting sessions with the spiritual guide.

Th next morning however Bhaiya confessed that he had been honestly worried. On Thursday nights he would stand in front of the window, looking up to the skies and pray. Following Thursday after our tire changing ordeal Bhaiya requested me to stand next to him while he prayed. I wondered why he had chosen me and for what purpose was I being asked to be by his side. While he was praying silently, I too closed my eyes and began praying. When his prayers were completed, he turned towards me with his palms held up and he looked at me. Then with both his palms he wiped his face; a typical Islamic ritual.

He then explained why he had asked me pray with him. "Ali you know why I did all of this. You have a noorani (radiant) face. I have also observed that you say your prayers regularly, and I want you by my side every Thursday." This revelation made my bond with Bhaiya even stronger and I even felt closer to him. He really loved me like his son.

Ever since I was a child in Bombay, I had a weak digestive system which often resulted in frequent loose motions and sometimes acute diarrhoea. This then entailed running to the bathroom perhaps eight or ten times a day which resulted in me becoming extremely weak. One morning I got up and felt the dreaded feeling in my stomach. I knew I was coming down with a bout of diarrhoea. The previous night Zaffar and I had eaten at a restaurant where the food was delicious but possibly not hygienic. By four in the afternoon I had broken all my previous records and had made fourteen visits to the restroom before the motions abated. Soon after I resembled a tuberculosis patient. I stayed home and Bhaby gave me some tablets which helped my condition.

When Zaffar came home, he told me that Afzalia wanted us to go to with him to 'Le Gourmet' that night even though he had told him about my condition, but Afzalia had still insisted Zaffar bring me along anyway."Zaffar look at me! Do you think, I have the strength to go to a nightclub?" I implored weakly. Zaffar replied that the previous night Afzalia had been at the club and had become friends with a Spanish girl from Barcelona who was the 'Main attraction'. Afzalia had told her he would very much like her to dance with me. She accepted but had told Afzalia that she was a professional dancer and a performing artist and that I would not be able to keep up with her. Afzalia took up the challenge on my behalf.

Bhaby of course was dead set against my going out in that weakened condition but Zaffar explained the situation to her and she finally accepted reluctantly. The only food I was able to eat for any form of nourishment was rice with curd which were easily digestible. Around 7.30 pm we dressed up, I in my semi-suit, which Afzalia had tailor-made for me, and Zaffar in one of his sleek suits. I asked Zaffar to pray for me as I felt I was being led to the alter to be sacrificed!

"Zaffar how does Afzalia expect me to dance in this condition and that too with a professional?" I asked earnestly.

"One round of my usual fast swing and I might faint," I added pitifully.

This girl from Barcelona was a Flamenco dancer. Those who have seen it know it is extremely fast-paced dance with its performers expected to move their feet vigorously and briskly. She was also known for dancing the rock and roll. Zaffar assured me to remain positive and kept on repeating "You can do it Ali!" This reminded me of the corner-men during boxing matches who continue to encourage and give instructions to their boxers even when he is about to lose. As Zaffar and I entered the club we saw that Afzalia was already seated at his regular table which happened to be the best in the club. He was happy to see me and began telling me about the challenge he had accepted. Meanwhile I was wondering to myself how he had not noticed my thin, drawn in and sunken cheeks. But this was obviously not on his mind. Instead he told me to show the Spanish dancer what rock and roll is all about and to let her take this experience with her to Spain. I merely shook my head.

Afzalia called the waiter and asked me what I wanted to drink. I requested the waiter to make me a big glass of sweet lassi (sweet buttermilk). This was to give me some strength without causing an upset stomach. Afzalia was sipping his scotch while Zaffar was having his beer. I kept on saying to them I hoped I don't let Afzalia down. Zaffar as usual was the cheerleader giving me confidence and Afzalia in his usual soft voice encouraged me.

The main attraction was announced and suddenly there she was with her partner; a striking-looking couple indeed. The dancing duo bowed as the guests welcomed them with their loud claps and their band started playing. The flamenco guitar - the most important instrument to accompany Spanish dancing - began strumming at an incredible speed and soon other instruments joined in to create a loud, fast pulsating symphony which took over the hall.

The female dancer with concave shells in her hands clapped quickly in rhythm and in sync with the drums which made my feet start tapping on the floor. Her extravagant costume included a long skirt with a four feet trailing train made up of colourful, flowing ruffles. The top it off a vibrantly colourful shawl was tied around her waist to perfect the colour coordination of the whole ensemble.

The tall thin male dancer was clad in tight, black fitting pants, a white shirt and a short black vest. The rhythmic, vigorous dancing and strident tapping footwork was infectious and soon I too was tapping my feet on the floor while sitting and waiting. The flamenco was a dance which I was witnessing for the first time. Perfecting the steps must take years of practice I thought to myself and hence felt confronted with a real challenge. The couple on the floor glided like the wind with such precision and grace and dazzled the audience and left everyone breathless.

After the scintillating dance the performers went backstage changed and came out to mingle with the guests. The bailaora (female flamenco dancer) joined us at our table while the bailaor had gathered around his own fans. Afzalia introduced us and the Latin beauty smiled and said hello. "He is a kid," she exclaimed, not in a derogatory way but as a mere observation while I sipped my lassi and also greeted her with a smile. I told her that was the first time I had ever witnessed flamenco dance and it was thrilling to watch and the two of them were awesome.

She glanced at my lassi and was more than ever convinced that I was a child drinking milk, unaware that poor me had literally just arisen from the dead. I explained to her about my fourteen visits to the washroom and that we use buttermilk to help us through the ordeal. She was intrigued and asked if I would be able to dance. I don't know I said but I am sure as hell going to give it my best.

I asked her if apart from the flamenco she danced to rock and roll music. "Oh yes!" she said exuberantly. "Since Bill Haley's rock and roll film showed in Europe, everyone had gone crazy man crazy!" she smilingly added in our dancing lingo. After she had a small peg to drink, Afzalia signaled his hand to the Le Gourmet band (it was prearranged by Afzalia) and the band started playing the One Two Three O'clock Rock. I said a silent prayer. "Oh God I need YOU now more than ever. Just do not let me faint. I rose and extended my hand to her. "Let's dance." I offered. "Let's," she replied.

I asked her to go to the end of the floor and start swaying to the music and I will join her, she was puzzled but obliged and went to the other end of the floor swaying to the music. As soon as she reached the other end she turned around to face where we were sitting, she saw me jump on the floor landing on my knees sliding towards her. When I was at her feet, I raised my hand to her, she held it and I got up and we started jiving. Then suddenly I did the back bend with my back touching the floor, she asked me what she should do. I told her just hold my hand while I got up slowly. Now I began my signature steps, with my bent knees swinging her left and right really fast with two steps to every beat, I thought if I continued, I might faint. But luckily, she stopped me because she couldn't keep up with me and told me that I was "something else and that she couldn't keep up with me." She hugged me and kissed me on the cheeks.

The guests all rose up and continued clapping and we both gave a bow and approached Afzalia and Zaffar at the table. "Afzal, you were right. Ali is really a great dancer." Afzalia with a big smile said ,"I told you so." Zaffar told her Ali also taught me how to dance. Afzalia ordered one more round of drinks for the three of them. I signalled the waiter with my glass. "I must know if Ali is not allowed to drink," our Spanish guest genuinely asked.

"I see that he only drinks milk all the time," she added. We laughed and I told her again about my loose motions and the ensuing weakness. "Oh Dios mio!" She exclaimed in Spanish. "It's amazing with all of that going on you were able to dance like that! What would you have done to me if you were not sick! "she exclaimed striking her forehead. Zaffar mustered up courage and danced with her the slow fox trot until the second flamenco performance.

They changed into another colourful costume and pleased the crowd with another great performance. While dancing she kept on looking at us all the time and smiling. With Afzalia's charm, smile and spending habits all lady artists used to fall for him. It was a great and memorable night although I don't remember the name of the Spanish girl. By the time we left Afzalia was drunk. Aslam the driver took us home. Zaffar and I put Afzalia to bed at his home and he kept repeating "Ali you were great" and fell asleep like a baby.

Aslam then dropped us to our home, and we entered the house, from the back door. Bhaiya was busy writing as usual, and Bhaby was waiting for us to see if I was in one piece. She sat with us in our bedroom while Zaffar told her in detail about the evening. "Ali I really don't understand how you do this," is all Bhaby said and I was listening to all this half asleep. Next morning it was my turn to take the kids to school and for once Zaffar helped me otherwise it was always the other way around.

Zaffar had been suffering from haemorrhoids for a long time and now they had begun bleeding profusely accompanied by a lot of pain. Every time he went to pass stool he would bleed even more with unbearable pain. The proctologist who had treated him since his ailment advised him to have an operation. He recommended one of the top surgeons and the date was set. "Ali please be with me in the hospital till I fully recover," Zaffar implored. "Zaffar, do you have to ask this? You know I will always gladly be there for you as you have been there for me," I replied genuinely.

Zaffar was admitted to a hospital and on the day of surgery Bhaby was there with all the brothers present with her. I must confess Bhaby always loved Zaffar and me like her sons and she would do anything for us. If you saw Zaffar he was tough as they come but when in pain he was worse than a baby. However, I don't blame him for those days after surgery they inserted a round thin plastic tube to ensure the wound did not stick together which was really very painful which the doctor had informed us before the surgery. Nowadays with advanced technology after surgery for haemorrhoids removal there is a procedure called rubber band ligation which is painless, and the patient can go home the same day. Still some patients did suffer from pain.

Zaffar had to stay in the hospital for at least five days for the wound to heal before he would be released. When the attendants brought Zaffar to his hospital bed he was moaning even though they had given him morphine for his pain. Everyone tried to calm him but to no avail. Bhaby asked the nurse if they could give him an extra dose but she replied they had already given him the maximum amount. The Imam brothers and Bhaby all left at five p.m. as the visiting hour was over. I was allowed to stay to take care of Zaffar during the night.

I sat on a quite comfortable chair thinking I could spend the rest of the night snuggled in it. As the effect of the morphine wore out the pain intensified, and I could not bear to see Zaffar suffer so much. I felt helpless as there was nothing I could do. Finally, I climbed into the bed half lying down and half sitting held Zaffar's head into my arms thinking he might feel some comfort in that position. However, that did not help, and the pain kept increasing and I could see that he was turning blue with excruciating pain.

Zaffar pleaded with me to ask the nurse to give him another shot. I placed his head gently on the pillow and rushed to call the nurse. She arrived with another dose and administered it to him. It gradually took effect and reduced the pain about seventy percent. I took my position in the bed and Zaffar napped for a while like a baby in my arms and then awoke. "Ali the pain is gradually coming back, please tell the nurse to give me another shot." The nurse apologized and said she could not give another shot so soon.

She returned with me to the room and asked if Zaffar smoked. I replied that he did. "That is why the morphine is not helping him as much as it should," the nurse explained. The kind nurse further revealed to us that Zaffar would have to try and bear the pain as an extra dose at such little intervals could cause some dangerous reaction.

I did not sleep the entire night, not even a wink. In the morning Bhaby came to visit and I told her of the difficult night Zaffar had endured. She suggested I go home; takes shower; eat; sleep and return after I had rested. She added that on my return I should bring back sandwiches a large flask of tea for the two of us for later. I was exhausted when the driver took me home and I was dozing off. "Ali sahab if I have to brake suddenly you will fall on to the street!" he implored.

The issue was that the passenger-side door of the van was damaged and could not be drawn shut properly, and in those days there was no seat belts. It reminded me of the time I was teaching Eddie to drive, and he had accidentally braked and I had fallen off the van. Luckily the van was moving slowly. With great difficulty I kept awake until we reached home. I took my shower, ate and napped. By the time I woke up, the flask of tea and snacks had been prepared. I changed and immediately returned to the hospital.

Bhaby informed me that Zaffar had been in pain the whole day and had complained about the hospital food.

Bhaby left at five in the afternoon and I took over the night shift. Bhaiya and family were kept abreast of Zaffar's progress by Bhaby from her visit. Bhaiya also used to call the hospital and speak to me. He loved Zaffar a lot as he was the youngest and was treated like a son. Zaffar enjoyed the egg sandwich and tea which brought back some colour to his face. We both spent another three nights in the hospital. The pain was slowly but surely subsiding and Zaffar could now sit up in bed, adjusting his bottom to the most comfortable position for him. The surgeon made daily rounds to check the healing from the surgery. "Zaffar, you can now go home in two days" the doctor encouragingly reassured. Meanwhile I used to flirt with the nurse who didn't seem to mind.

Bhaiya came with Bhaby to take us home. When we arrived Mazhar Abba helped me to take Zaffar into the house. Zaffar walked awkwardly because he was still in pain although the doctor reassured us that Zaffar's discomforting condition would completely heal gradually. Zaffar was given medicine to soften his stool and ointment to apply twice daily. Within a week Zaffar was himself again and he thanked me profusely. "Ali, I could not have gone through this surgery without you. Thank you!" Zaffar enthused. "Arey yaar Zaffar, you would have done the same for me," I replied. Zaffar jokingly added that he had felt that I could never be serious as he had seen me flirting with the nurse. We both had a laugh together over this.

After nearly a week Zaffar returned to the office and life went on the same routine except now there were no late nights out for the time being.

Bhaiya was also busy interviewing crew for the movie and I was waiting anxiously for my next role in my life filled with its ups and downs.

Meanwhile Musti and I continued to go with Susie and family for our regular jaunts to Clifton Beach in the evenings after dinner. Zaffar sometimes joined us but poor Susie's Daddy, never d1d. I used to have regular arguments with Susie because she was over-possessive and jealous. But I was admittedly never a one girl guy even during my romance with my true love Nosrat.

Susie used to make sure her friends would spy on me and report back to her if they saw me at jam sessions with other girls. When she came to the jam sessions then I was with Susie only and everything was okay. Once I got really angry and told Susie that was the end of our relationship as I didn't like to be bogged down. I eventually stopped going to her house.

Musti kept calling me and when we met, he advised me to forgive her as she loved me a lot, he claimed. Of course, I knew that but enough is enough. Eddie on the other hand never interfered even though he was with us all the time.

By now Susie had become very close to Hamid Mamoo at Maritime. She would continue to call him and complain to him about my endless flirting and she would beg that I forgave her and go back to her. Hamid Mamoo would reassure her in his soft soothing voice he would talk to me which he did. I explained to him that I had always had a fun and flirtatious nature and that I thought I could never change. Susie continued to pester Hamid Mamoo but this time, while sobbing she requested him to tell me that she was very sorry. I had never met anyone as patient as Hamid Mamoo. If I was in his place, I would have told her to stop calling. "Ali please for my sake go to Susie's house because she was crying and pleading." Hamid Mamoo implored.

I called Musti and we went to her house. Eventually though, once I got so fed up and could not bear it anymore. I had had enough of this drama and got up to leave for good. Three weeks had passed, and I had moved on with my life as usual. Susie continued to call poor Hamid Mamoo, Musti and even Mazhar Abba who tried their best to calm her down. I told Hamid Mamoo to please convince her that it was really finally over. Susie was stubborn and in love and she continued calling Musti as she knew she could depend on him as he was her good friend since school days. "Ali come with me for the last time," Musti pleaded. "If it does not work out this time, I will never force you again," he added.

The following Saturday Musti and I had a night out and I went to his house to stay the night. In the morning we had our breakfast (or rather brunch) and the headed to Susie's house. On the way we had picked up Zaffar who was eager to see the outcome. She opened the door and tried to hug me but I shrugged her off. Her mum and Deborah had gone to the synagogue and Baby was feeding their dad. We sat down in their living room and Susie began crying, apologizing for her jealous behaviour. But it was the same script being repeated. I advised her that we should both move on with our lives.

Suddenly she got up (as God is my witness) and fell to my feet. I pushed her away, and in hindsight, cruelly told her to stop acting as the camera was not on her, but she held on sobbing. Zaffar and Musti told me to have some heart and feeling as Susie was sincerely sorry. I picked her up hugged her and told her that I liked her a lot but I valued my freedom more, and that she should be patient. She nodded agreeably and that was a happy ending.

We continued going to jam sessions. The emcee announced that the following Sunday the club would be introducing a live band on trial basis and that the entry fees would be increased a little.

Nobody had any objections as we all waited excitedly for Sunday to arrive. It so happened that an American ship had docked at Karachi port. Naturally the sailors were in town looking around shopping for their loved ones an discovering the city. A group of five Americans sailors saw the flag outside the jam session hall and entered, surprised and delighted, as they did not expect jams and dancing to take place in Karachi.

They danced with the local girls who were excited to interact with them as never in their wildest dreams would they have gotten such an opportunity. The sailors admirably behaved like gentlemen with the girls. The emcee welcomed the honoured guests and with great applause everyone stood up clapping. "We will now have the Rock and Roll competition," the emcee announced excitedly. "Will our honoured guests please be the judges?" he added. The sailors stood up and bowed. Three of the sailors were Africa- American while the remaining two were Caucasian.

The band started with a Big Bang. The throbbing of the cymbals and the pulsating beat were so loud and filled the hall with a thrilling energy we had never experienced in the previous sessions. The band was here to stay. The band consisted mostly of Catholic boys who were smart and talented enough to prove themselves. For the opening number they picked Bill Haley's 'One, Two Three O'clock Rock.' I thought that was a smart move and everyone was at their best. After all they had to prove that they were no less than the Americans at dancing.

Every five minutes one of the judges would get up and pat the shoulder of a couple and politely apologize, signalling their elimination. After nearly forty-five minutes of dancing Shafi and I were left as usual. I had saved a couple of my steps for the last dance. The band played again from the film 'Rock Around The Clock' equally fast like the previous time. Thelma and I started from the opposite side of the hall, while Shafi danced in the center of the dance floor. As soon as Thelma approached me, I picked her up and swung her up around my shoulders. As soon as she landed, I turned around and went sliding between her feet and stood up dancing up a frenzy with her.

My feet were moving really fast while simultaneously swinging her to and fro; left to right without letting go, then performing a back bend. Then I moved away from her and when I was at a distance I came running and threw myself on the floor, sliding on my knees with my head practically touching the floor and went under her spread legs to the other side of her. The music stopped and after about a minute one of the judges came to us and raising my hand with Thelma's declared us champions. The judge then very seriously suggested that I should go to Hollywood.

Zaffar and Musti were also with us at the jam session as was George after a long time. He approached us and asking me for a favour. "Ali, please don't refuse," George implored. I assured him that I would if I could, I would do my best. "Do you know a girl called Lilly." George asked hopefully. I closed my eyes thinking of all the girls I knew but I couldn't pinpoint her. "Sorry pal. I don't think I know her," I replied. George then went on to describe her in detail to me. "Oh yeah," I said." She usually hangs out with four girls who always sit together." "Ali, I love her very much, but I don't have the guts to go and express my deep feelings," George said. "Can you please talk to her on my behalf?"

I told George that I would convey his feelings to her but warned him that Lilly was little bit flirt and could he handle that. He was confident that after she finds out about his love for her, she will change. I told him to come again next Sunday and I would talk to her then. After the jam session I went with Musti and Zaffar to Metropole's bar and lounge. Musti ordered cold beers and for snacks there were always salty and spicy nuts on hand.

After the first beer, Musti shook his head in pity and said, "Poor George! He has really fallen head over heels for Lilly."

The following Sunday we went to the jam session and as usual girls would come and try to reserve the next dance with me. While dancing I approached where Lilly was seated and told her that I will dance the next slow number with her. All the girls at her table were smiling and I'm sure they were telling Lilly that I am definitely interested in her. On the next slow dance, she was already standing and waiting for me. "Oh, Ali I'm so excited that you showed interest in me for I really want to be your girl." "Woh! Hold your horses" I said and laughed and told her about George and how deeply he truly he loved her.

Lilly turned her head towards our table and saw Zaffar, Musti, Thelma and George. I told her to look at the extreme left. She said she'd seen him watching her all the time and commented that she thought he was a gentle soul. "Lilly, George is a good-looking shy boy and he is not interested in anybody but you," I said emphatically. "Okay I will give it a shot," she acquiesced. But before I introduced them, I warned her about one more thing." Lilly you cannot just play around with him," I said.

"Go out with two or three times. See how you feel about him and then became his gal. Once you feel you really like him and want to be with him without the need to flirt around with others as before, only then commit." She agreed, and I took her over to our table. George was so eager that before we reached our table he stood up and pulled out a chair waiting for us to approach. Like a thorough gentleman he politely offered the chair for her to sit on. I introduced them and then Lilly said she would return after going to her friends to tell them that she would be joining us. She was happy with George's initial reaction.

She was equally happy that she was now part of our crowd. I noticed that she spoke to George very sweetly, while his eyes were transfixed on her, like he was in some kind of a trance. I had never seen him so happy before. He was so engrossed with Lilly as if we did not even exist! I too was happy for them. I hoped she would not break his heart. A friend like Musti is hard to come by. Suddenly he told me to go on with Zaffar while he was taking George and Lilly to dinner at the Palace Hotel lounge. The new couple were overwhelmed and overjoyed.

I kept seeing George and Lilly together a couple of times dancing cheek to cheek on slow dances and it seemed this romance is going to go the distance. They looked genuinely happy. I asked Lilly about their relationship and she told me not to worry as it was going great which put my mind at ease. It was really wonderful to see them happy. He was not rich but he would go out of his way to shower on her gifts; the usual romantic boy and girl stuff. After about month and a half George called me with a sense of great urgency in his voice. " Ali sorry for bothering you but I must see you. It's important."

I replied I couldn't right away as I was going to Le Gourmet with Zaffar. He pleaded and asked if he could join us. I asked Zaffar and he gladly gave his consent. We found George waiting for us at the gates of Palace Hotel.

While Zaffar parked George joined us. He wanted to lay out his problems right away there and then. "George, hold it take it easy!" I guffawed "We have the whole night to discuss. Let's have a drink." After a drink he unloaded all that he had been carrying around within for a couple of days. "Ali Lilly just dropped me for someone else," George said helplessly with a very sad and unhappy voice.

I asked him who the other fellow was but George didn't know his name but knew he was a rich guy who had a nice Chevy. I asked Zaffar if he knew the guy, but he too didn't. Our photographer friend Razi also had no clue. But the ambitious flirt Lilly went where the money was. She had broken promise to me. I was mad oh! fuming mad. George said that Lilly's new friend was not even nice looking. I got so angry if she was there, I would have slapped her. We had all had too many drinks just to down George's sorrows.

The next morning was a Sunday. After breakfast I took a pen and a pad in the quiet of our room, with Zaffar on his bed relaxing. In my anger I began writing a derogatory poem about girls, in light of what Lilly had done to George. I told Zaffar to keep on relaxing and not to disturb me. The angry lines started overflowing - with the title: 'Love is Fraud' (poem next page)

I was surprised that I had just written a poem; a talent I did not know I had. All thanks to Lilly. In hindsight I am reminded of the quote by English poet William Wordsworth: "Poetry is the spontaneous overflow of powerful feelings: it takes it origins from emotion recollected in tranquility." The words of my poem are indeed harsh. But please bear in mind I was seventeen and very angry and of course all girls are not the same. I sincerely hope that any girl who reads will understand that I had vented out my anger in this poem.

I read it to Zaffar. "Ali I just cannot believe you just wrote a poem," he enthused incredulously. I told him he was not alone as I was surprised as he was. I realized then that you cannot just sit and start writing a poem. Something needs to inspire. The next morning in office I asked Naseem sahab the typist to type five copies of 'Love is Fraud'. He read it smiling shook his head. I then showed it to Hamid Mamoo, who asked me encouragingly how many hidden talents I had.

"You have handled your shipping job well. You are the king of dancing, and now a poet too." he added that my words were very harsh and not all girls were like that and I reassured him that I was aware of that. I explained to Hamid Mamoo that the words had just kept flowing out in anger and that I had not even made an effort. I added that I hoped in future I would be inspired to write more poems.

LOVE IS FRAUD

If love is what love I've seen I don't think love had ever been In this world full of girls Who run for money, jewels, and pearls.

Have you heard of that word 'love' From inscrutable dames who like a dove? Riches, luxury, sex like fire All they have is ready for hire.

Rotten are they to the very core Not a soul could detect it before Heart and mind fraud and fake Still the men are eager to take.

Sweet is the nectar, stings the bee Underneath the sweet face you cannot see Solemn oaths; an artistic act Inurnment of deed with great tact.

So see, you my fellows with a lonely heart Unreliable were women from the very start.

Samson too lost his strength of pride Intoxicated Delilah took him for a ride.

Ever they will be unfaithful.

At the next jam session, I was with my usual friends, including, of course George. Munna had also joined us. I showed the poem to all of them, and they were all surprised at how I had managed this fitting poem so quickly. In fact, they all agreed that she deserved it. Lilly came with her quartet of friends, and what looked like her new boyfriend. Somehow, he seemed like a fish out of water and did not know in the least how to mix in this crowd.

I gave a copy to my friends to read. And, then, I walked up to Lilly and threw the poem on her face, and said, "This is for you, you tramp. I will make sure that you don't get to dance with the boys in our sessions." And once I told them about her, hardly anyone danced with her. She was not seen in future jam sessions. And meanwhile, when the boys finished reading the poem, they all congratulated me, and Thelma even said, "Ali, I am not like that. I have a boyfriend since a long time." I told her, "I know, I know. You don't have to tell me that. It's not for all girls; it was a spur of the moment thing."

The girls came and George said, "Since my problems inspired this, can I keep a copy?" "Of course, you can. I meant to give you one copy." I still have one of the copies, also of the poems which followed after that.

Today, as I am writing this, I am still reminiscing those days. Teenage years are one of the most trying times of our lives as our hormones are rushing, there is an anguish of uncertainty, the pressure of peer competition. This becomes all too much for a teenager to handle; it affects all of us, some more some less. Most of all, we spend time contemplating in solitude, thinking what does the future has in store for us.

One night, the band leader of the night club announced about the coming attraction. Six teenage girls were coming from Sydney, Australia. They had a unique talent for performing the French Cancan dance on roller skates. Zaffar and I were with Afzalia at the night club, and Afzalia said, "This would be very interesting for you, Ali. During my visit to Paris, I have seen the Cancan, but never heard of, on skates. It should be good."

The following week, Zaffar reminded me of the Cancan, and we went to Le Gourmet that night. Before the main attraction, the four girls were sitting with their chaperon, a lady with glasses, grey hair, and with the looks of a strict teacher in school. She looked very serious and was suited for the job. The main attraction was announced, the girls came screaming with a jump and fell to the floor with splits and rose up with ease.

Their dresses were in different colours, multi-layered, and full of frills and ruffles on their petticoats. And with it, they wore a black pantyhose, or fishnet stockings. It was a very lively dance with high kicks in unison and lifting up of the skirts as they moved from left to right, exposing their legs and petticoats. The amazing thing was it was all done on roller skates, which was an amazing difficult feat. Everyone who witnessed it were very impressed.

One great advantage we had over other guests was that Afzalia was a big spender with a golden generous heart, and the management made sure that he had the best of everything. This included the performers who were ushered to his table first. The waiters served him well. And, he was a regular. He brought all the Japanese and European guests, who were the principals of various shipping companies, to the club. That meant great business for the night club. It was natural that he was the most valuable customer for them and was treated like a royal.

While the girls were performing, I requested Afzalia to tell the manager to bring the girls to our table after the performance. He just waved at the manager, who came running, and Afzalia whispered in his ear. The manager nodded, smiled, and went away. He went behind the curtains and waited. The girls changed and came to our table with their chaperon. He introduced Afzalia, and they already knew he was the guest to please.

Afzalia introduced Zaffar, and then said to them, "Let me introduce Ali, the king of rock and roll." And the chaperon introduced the girls. Dorothy, Esther, Pam, and I cannot remember the other girl's name. Right away, Dorothy caught my eye, although Esther was prettier and was eyeing me. Zaffar got interested in Pam, and they seemed to be busy talking to one another. Afzalia was smart; he knew the chaperon was here to keep all in check, so he kept on talking about Australia.

I got up and requested the band for a slow one. I asked Dorothy to dance, she accepted; and Zaffar took Pam to the floor. We were dancing cheek to cheek, and the eyes of the chaperon were watching us like a hawk. Esther danced with one of the guests, and Afzalia was keeping the old lady busy. I also danced with Esther, and she held on to me tight, pressing herself to me.

I did not mind, and I kept reminding myself, 'I have to be very tactful, not to complicate things.' I asked Dorothy if she would meet us down in the compound of the hotel in the morning, but they were not allowed to go out without the chaperon. I called Musti, and told him about the girls, and he agreed to pick us up at home. We met him after breakfast, on the way to the hotel.

I explained to Musti about Esther and told him that he should keep her busy so I could whisk Dorothy away. It worked! Zaffar was with Pam, and Musti was doing a good job keeping her busy, telling her stories about Kuwait, and more. I went with Dorothy to the other end of the gardens, and we were already kissing and necking. Dorothy told me about her family, and I told her about mine. It was a different kind of feeling, for it was my first experience with a foreigner girl, and it was great.

Musti called me the next day. "Ali", he said, "this Esther has fallen head over heels, and she told me that she loved you at first sight. Knowing you, I pity the poor girl. On the one hand, you are very close to Susie, on the other hand, this Dorothy, and on top of that, Esther. God help you." Musti was right, but I could not help it as that is the way it was. Maybe one fine day when I get married, I might settle down. Even then, I am afraid, I might waver from the straight path. I hope not.

My spare time between my regular work was for Susie and Dorothy, but now, more time was for Dorothy. She was a simple, sweet girl; not very beautiful, but I liked her a lot. The chaperon found out about our meetings in the gardens and she scolded her like a child. On their day off, we went to see a movie. April Love was playing in the Rex theater, with Pat Boone and Shirley Jones. The girls were naturally accompanied by the chaperon.

By now, the old lady was friendly with me, because I had buttered her up, and she would allow me to be with Dorothy. I sat between Dorothy and Esther; Zaffar was seated between her and Pam, and then there was the other girl and the chaperon. I was busy with Dorothy, doing what teenagers did in the movie with their gals, and Esther was squeezing my other hand. I was young and human, so I started my affair on the quiet with Esther.

The affair had to end, because the time of the contract was over, and the girls were going back to Sydney. They were all packed up, and I waited in the lounge to bid farewell to all. I always hated goodbyes, especially when saying goodbye to family or loved ones. Esther came much before them, for she knew my farewell with Dorothy would last long. She hugged me, kissed me, and would not let me go. Then the chaperon came down.

She hugged me and Zaffar, with a slight smile on her face. Zaffar and Pam, too, hugged. Pam used to always complain to me, "Your friend is so shy; he is such a gentleman that I had to initiate the kiss always." I smiled and said, "Yep, that is him." And, the last to come down was Dorothy. She had a white Burkha - the Hijab - which covered the whole body. The eyes were covered with white net, enabling a woman to see through it.

Of course, that is not the actual Hijab, for Gods' guidance is a lady should cover the head with a big scarf, and the ends of the scarf should come down to cover the breasts. Her arms should be covered, with the exception of the hands, and face should not be covered. All countries had created their own Hijabs, making it very inconvenient for the ladies.

Dorothy had bought the Burkha as a souvenir, when she approached me, she pulled me against her, and covered both of us with the Burkha. We were kissing in the lounge, holding on tight to each other. Everyone's luggage was loaded, and they were waiting for Dorothy. Pam came in and was pulling both of us. She gave me her address and made promises to write regularly.

With Dorothy out of the picture, I could now spend more time with Susie. And, as I spent more time with her, I was beginning to like her more and more. She was a beautiful girl; she proved to me that I was the only guy in her life. And then, there were the Friday dinners. Not caring what others would say, she would fill my plate with chicken pieces, even as I would insistently tell her that I didn't want her embarrassing herself in front of her family.

During working hours, whenever I was out running errands for Sanlay bhaiya, I used to make a quick stop at her house. She would be alone with her Dad, who was relaxing or sleeping. And, like mischievous teenagers, we used to kiss and caress, whispering, lest her dad would wake up. I found myself falling in love with her. Love - despite a string of pretty companions - it mostly seemed to elude the lifelong romance which was going to be ours. Now I was, to my surprise I was only hers. I was plunging into happiness, and later, into anger and repentance, which I was destined to experience with her as part of life.

One summer afternoon, she called me at the office. "Can you come home? We will have the whole house to ourselves", she said. I took permission form Afzalia, who said, "Go, it's okay. If Sanlay bahiya asks, I will tell him you are out, running errands for me." I rushed to her house, and before we could say anything, we were smooching and perspiring between each smooch. We were now both out of control, and our passion took over - we slept together - it was a first, for both of us, a rapture which cannot be explained in words. One has to experience it. All my life I never took advantage of any girls, their honour was important for me.

Before I could reach the final rapture, I had the sense and control to withdraw from a situation which could have posed a lot of anxiety and fear for us. She was virgin and, so, she started bleeding. We both worried it would not stop. She went to the bathroom and washed herself with cold water, and finally came out relieved.

I have always conducted my behaviour according to my conscience, and never once it was silent. But we were two young passionate people who were left alone; it was bound to happen. So now, I made it my mission to be with her alone, and love her and, never give her any more reason to be unhappy. I came back to the office, and Hamid Mamoo said, "Ali, I see something in your face I have never seen before. It's a kind of guilt." During lunch, Zaffar, Hamid Mamoo, and I went to the cafeteria, and I confided in full details of what just happened.

Both of them said, "Ali yaar, you should have controlled yourself, even if she could not." I said, "I know, I know. But now, I cannot reverse it." Mamoo said, "Ali, I hope you will not trouble this girl any more with all your shenanigans, for we do know you are notorious." I assured him that I had already made up my mind to not hurt her in anyway. That evening at home, Mazhar abba, took me aside in his room, and said, "I overheard what Mamoo and Zaffar were talking. Beta, you should know that all actions in life have consequences, and it's your duty to stand by her through thick and thin, and to marry her at the right time." Abba loved me like his son, I just hung my head low and nodded.

At the end of the day what counts is how you take the inventory of your relationship, what you learn from it, and how you turn into a better person. And I think I was trying to be a better person. I was praying that nobody would come and break my resolution. I had planned to get married, but that was easier said than done. It was kind of a wishful idea.

At that time, I was earning 150 rupees a month, and had no place of my own. But the biggest hurdle would be to get her parents' approval. I knew they would never agree for they always planned to get her married to a rich Jewish guy. Any parent would want their child to settle well. So, marriage was out for the time being. This reminded me of Nosrat and her mum.

We said, "Let's have fun and not load our teenage minds with big responsibility." Now, whenever we met, we had fun, like husband and wife. We met as often as she could get out of the house, and made love without any guilt, and this also was a new experience. My brother-in-law Mohammad, husband of my sister Firouze (now separated) lived in a small tiny house, just opposite our house. It was only a walk across the street. He lived with his, mum and during the day, they were both at work. I had a spare key, and I used to meet Susie there in complete privacy.

The movie's script was ready, and so was the crew for making the movie. Now, Bhaiya was going to Lahore frequently for negotiations with the actors. You know how it works - the actors would try to ask for more and more, while Bhaiya had a fix sum in mind for each. The leading lady was Meena Shori, who was famous in Indian films, and who is still remembered for her famous song Laralapa. The old timers still remember her by that name. She was now settled in Pakistan and was successful in Lahore films.

Then there was another giant of an actor, Himalya Walla, who was also from Indian cinema. He was a tall man with a gruff voice, well-known for his villainous roles. He appeared dangerous on screen but was a nice and sweet man in real life. He and Meena were the highest paid actors of our movie. Then, there was the hero of the film, Ejaz

Durrani, a tall handsome man, who was a newcomer to the filmy world.

Back in Karachi, Bhaiya had a long meeting with Sanlay bhiya and Afzalia, who were the only financiers of this venture, but had no clue about films. They finally summoned Mazhar Abba, and me in the cabin. Bhaiya looked at us with a big smile of satisfaction on his face, and said, "Our film company has been established in the name of Movie Makers Ltd. I am the Managing Director, and Sanlay bhaiya and Afzlia are Directors." Mazhar abba was appointed as the production manager, and I was his assistant.

We were both employees of the company. Mazhar abba got an increase in salary, and I, was employed with an initial salary of 150 rupees, which was 25 more than I was earning in Maritime.

Sanlay bhaiya made sure that he was also the Comptroller, for he could never let anyone handle the financial aspect of this big venture. And rightfully so, for Afzalia was a darling spendthrift, and Bhaiya never handled money before and that too an amount this big. The following day, Bhaiya, abba, and I went to the Eastern Film Studios to finalize which office we would rent, and to get introduced to the owner of the Studios.

He was a fair chubby guy; his name was Sayeed Haroon. Bhaiya introduced abba and me and said, "This is Ali Reza, who, also is an Iranian." I spoke to him in Farsi. He was not fluent, but he could carry a conversation. We hit it off right away; we would become best friends. The office we got was the biggest in the studio, for no other production company had a big project like ours. The movie that Bhaiya had in mind would go on to become the most expensive Pakistani movie of our time.

Saeed called his assistant to our office and instructed him to get it furnished and ready by next week, and said, "If these gentlemen need anything, give them top priority." That made us confident that we would get priority in getting a sound stage for shooting and all other facilities of the studio at our convenience.

Up until now, not everything in life had turned out to be the way I wanted it, but I had fought; I had tried my best. I took a road that I knew nothing about, not knowing where I was headed. But I had reached my final destination, and now was time for the long-awaited celebration. I had arrived. I was in the film industry, which was my love.

My first job was to keep on going to the studio, after dropping the back kids to school. I was there to make sure that they had started furnishing the office, as promised. From there, I used to go to Muhammadi house, for as our office was still not ready, that's where the crew - Noor Mohammad Charlie, director; Mohib, director of photography; Jilani, the cameraman; Afzal, the music director, and our publicist Khizar Dehlavi — was invited.

Afzalia and Sanlay bhaiya's presence completed the backbone of the film.

Sanlay bhaiya had arranged for the Bihari cook, from Haleem Sahb's house, and I tell you, we had some delectable and delicious meals. After dinner, while tea was being served, Bhiaya stood up and announced, our movie will be named Sitaron ki Duniya, with Meena Shori and Ejaz in the lead, and Himalaya Walla as the big villain. And then, pointing at Charlie, he said "And, of course, our greatest and one and only, Noor Mohammad Sahab."

Finally, bhaiya introduced abba as the production manager and me as his assistant. Bhaiya asked the crew to be prepared for our meeting in the studio in a week. Before they left, copies of the script were given to Moheb sahab and Gilani. Khursheed, the music director, was at our house every day, from eleven in the morning till midnight. There were plans to include five or six songs in the movie, and they had to discuss the situation and timing when each song would be sung. Then, they had to decide the lyrics and the director who would work on the music. And of course, they had to decide whether it would be a sad song or a happy song. It was, indeed, a long process.

Even after spending a week on the songs, they were struggling with the lyrics. I think Khizr and some other person helped, and finally, Khursheed took the lyrics with him to make the final music, for had the playback singers waiting to record the songs. One month after the the dinner, we were ready for the Muharat — the first opening shot of the film. Meena and bhaiya had to shoot this scene. Mazhar abba had called Meena a week before the shoot to get a date from her. Luckily that went without a hitch, and we sent her round-trip ticket.

Mazhar Abba and I had selected a cook for our company. His job was to cook lunch, make tea, and snacks for about twenty-five people. For the main artists and crew, we had to order special food from top restaurants. I made sure that the sound stage had chairs so that important guests to sit and enjoy the shooting. Sanlay bhaiya and Afzalia came for the Muharat but were not constant visitors on the sets. The opening shot went well; both actors gave good performances. And Meena Shori, a veteran actor, established her experienced status from the first shot. She would definitely steal the show. The others were no match in front of her.

After everyone had had their lunch and had exchanged opinions regarding the shoot, Moheb called for pack up. Everyone gradually went their own way. I was lucky that Abba told me, "Ali drive Meenaji to her hotel." Throughout the drive, she was so friendly. She knew that I, like her, had come there from Bombay. She said, "Ali, tell me about your life in Bombay." I told her about my life in short. She said, "Ali, I am amazed at your courage, and I am genuinely glad for you. Work hard and you will go places in the industry, although our film industry is nothing compared to India."

Our office at the studio was now ready. Abba and I went there to give it the finishing touch, and also took with us regular office stationery, like note pads, pens and pencils. We set up the telephone on the desk. We also placed in the office a large couch in the anticipation that it would help if and when one had to sleep the night there. We went to Kodak and picked up five rolls of negatives, for we were to start shooting in full swing. We then stored those rolls in the studio's cold storage.

Abba arranged two tickets for Meena and Ejaz, reserved hotel rooms for them. There was no more Maritime office for me. I missed it, of course, but felt happier in our studio office. Shooting of two films was in progress at the time, but their names escape me now. The heroine of one of them was Shamim Ara, also a newcomer. She was about five three, had a dark complexion but a nice face. Saeed had also introduced me to a sound engineer, a tall and chubby Baluchi guy with receding curly hair.

Even he spoke a little Farsi. We liked one another right away, and now I had two friends here who could speak Farsi and that made me feel at home in the studios. His name escapes me, I think it was Rasool. I went on the set of one of the films, and Rasool introduced me to Shamim Ara, the director, and the camera man. I was given royal treatment for the main reason that I was with Movie Makers, a name which was now a big news in the industry. This was possible through the entertainment newspapers.

I was seated right behind the camera man, and this was the first time I was seeing a shot as an important guest. I had seen a couple of film shootings in Bombay. I remember the first one. It was in the rainy season; I was about twelve, and I saw Dev Anand and Soraya, a top actress and singer of her time, shooting. But, back then, I had to stand way back for the person who took me in was a nobody.

Anyway, after the shot was over, I went and sat in our office. After a little while, Shamim came in. I jumped up, surprised and offered her a seat. She was very friendly and said. "So, you are Ali Reza, the king of rock and roll." I was surprised and asked, "How do you know?" She told me that she had read about me in entertainment news and had also read that I would be dancing in Sitaron ki Duniya.

Oh boy! Boy oh boy! I was so happy! I started smiling sheepishly, and told her, "Yes, that's true. And, I will also have my first scene, acting with Charlie Chaplin, the great." After we chatted a little more, one of the assistants came to our office and said," Madame, the next shot is ready. You are wanted on the sets." She got up and left saying Ali hope we meet again.

The next day, I visited the sets where Susie was shooting. Her mum was seated behind the camera man, and I joined her. She always accompanied Susie and watched her like a hawk. And that was good actually, for the film industry people could not be trusted. Knowing Susie's mother was there with her put my mind at ease. Mum and I were seated next to each other and after every shot, they would come to our office and relax. I told Susie, "You are good at your work, and I am proud of you." This brought a big smile on her face. We all drank tea by the cups, for it was both relaxing and invigorating.

At home that night, bhaiya asked Abba, "Are you guys ready with all arrangements for our big day tomorrow? Abba answered, "Everything is arranged," and looking at me, said, "we are taking care of everyone and everything." I nodded and said, "Bhaiya, don't worry." I wanted to do this right. After all, bhaiya wore many caps, he was, at least to me, the director, producer, writer, and actor, and also had the added burden of supervising the director, who clearly need help. Later on, I used to wonder why bhaiya had chosen Moheb, for he was not very competent.

The day of our shooting finally arrived. Bhaiya, who used to go to bed at four a.m., went to bed early, and was up at six. We had an early breakfast, and I took him to the studios in our van. We were in the studio; Moheb and Gilani were there to meet him. Saeed was there to greet us and wish us good luck. I came back, driving fast to go home and pick up the kids to take them to school. Then, I came back and had some tea while Zaffar had his breakfast.

Zaffar drove to go to Maritime, while I closed my eyes in the van. I had a hectic day ahead, I realized, and that I should get as much rest as possible. After Zaffar got off, I took the van and went to Ejaz's hotel to pick him up. I called him from the lobby, but he asked me to come up to his room. As I entered, I saw he was still oiled and had not taken his shower. Worried, I said, "Ejaz, we will be late. You are not even dressed yet." But he replied, "Ali, don't worry. We will be on time. It takes long for them to get the studio ready for the shot."

Well, I was not yet familiar with how shooting worked, so I resigned to the fact thinking that he knew better. While he was still massaging his hair, he started telling me how he takes care of his hair with sarso — mustard — oil. It nourishes the roots of the hair and make them very healthy. When he was done, I saw his hair indeed looked silky and smooth, and he had slight waves. He looked great.

Ejaz was right. When we arrived at the studios, we went to the sound stage and saw Gilani and camera man Afzal checking all the lights. They kept focusing on the spot where the scene was to be enacted, directing each light man on the plank way above where to focus. "See what I told you, Ali?" Ejaz said. Indeed, I was learning fast.

Meena arrived later. Both artists sat in our office, going over the script. Moheb was instructing them at the same time, while Bhaiya was there, too. Believe it or not, the first shot was filmed successfully, and Moheb declared lunch time. While they were shooting, I rushed to town to pick up the special food from the top restaurant. Abba had made a contract with them for good food for the top artists, and they were very happy and proud they would be making food for movie stars.

I rushed back to the studios in time with food and was pleased to see the servants had already set the table. The food was not only for the stars, but also for Bhaiya, Gilani, Afzal, and Moheb. The rest of us, even Mazhar Abba, ate the bulk food, which was cooked, even Mazhar Abba. It was not the best quality but had plenty of meat. It was curry and nan bread.

The shoot lasted around ten days, but not a whole lot of work was done. This was because so many scenes needed five or six takes, sometimes even more. And this was because Ejaz could not get it right. Meena, on the other hand gave perfect takes from the very first shot. She was helpful and tried to encourage him by giving him guidance and confidence. She was a pro, and had a long resume, from Bombay and here. Ejaz had no expression on his face, but he tried his best to deliver his dialogues. The only thing to his credit was that he was strikingly handsome.

We finally packed up, and took both of them to the airport, for they had given dates to other directors in Lahore. In these ten days, I had learnt a lot. I was getting familiar, though in a hurry, about production under the guidance of Bhaiya. He had experience in production and acting from his days in Bihar. Abba was an experienced administrator, from the time in Maritime. Often, he was sent to take care of the branch in Chittagong and Dhaka. I immersed myself in the beauty of this opportunity, which had been my lifelong dream. So, the long hours it required did not discourage me in the least.

The following week, my time was spent in the studios with Afzal. He was trying to get the rushes ready. I made sure that he had everything, including snacks and tea. The rushes were ready, and on a Saturday, I had booked the projector hall, which was quite big, almost the size of a small theater. Our movie gang consisting of Bhaiya, Sanlay bhaiya, Afzalia, the full filming crew, bhabi, Zaffar, Mazhar abba, and some of their guests.

I instructed the kitchen to bring tea for everyone after the rushes, and then finally sat beside Zaffar to watch. Everyone was anxious, but Bhaiya was the most worried. His foremost worry was the reaction of Sanlay bhaiya and Afzalia. After all, they were the financers. Gilani looked up and called out to the projectionist to roll. The room lights were dimmed, and the rushes started. It was only one reel;

the filming was done expertly. Meena looked like her usual pretty self and displayed natural acting. Ejaz looked really handsome but delivered his dialogues like a statue.

Bhaiya, Mazhaar Abba, and I immediately looked towards Sanlay bhaiya and Afzal for approval. They had big smiles on their faces, and we let out a sigh of relief. They were happy for their elder brother knew what he was doing. They first of all congratulated Bhaiya, then they were full of praise for Gilani and Afzal for such good picturing, and lastly Moheb. Sanlay bhaiya added jokingly, "Hope it makes money."

From there, we were invited to Sanlay's for lunch, which was great. It had been prepared by the Bihari cook. I was the first to get the table laid, and the first thing I checked was whether there was Bihari kebab on the menu. There it was! It was a very satisfying day. The film rushes went great, and the dinner was scrumptious, absolutely mouth-watering delectable food to say the least.

I could not spend more time with my darling Susie anymore. Only now and then, I could spare time between my busy schedule. I would meet her in our private hide out. We were now really husband and wife, and these rendezvous that we had was the best relaxation. Now, I knew, I am in love with her after Nosrat. We started making plans of how to hurdle all the difficulties - and believe me they were too many - and get married at a later date.

When I was away from Susie, poems started coming in my mind, and the first one, which took me ten minutes - is as follows:

SUSIE MY LOVE

Sanguine are her tender lips A kiss, for a world, I would not miss Divine, lovely a heavenly bliss Adorable, possessive is her lasting kiss Her hair is black, silky and long My love for her is deep and strong Her eyes are kind and slightly brown They don't know what it is to frown.

Lavishly blessed with fabulous charms Unique is her grace in all her ways Could I bundle you in my longing arms I am ever yours, most warmly she says.

Combine her beauty, faith and grace All so clearly written on her face Exquisite like the heavens above Susie my darling you are my love.

Abba booked the sound stage for a second round of shooting, which was to start in a week. This time, the great villain Himalaya Walla was coming along with Meena and Ejaz. As usual, Abba arranged for tickets through our travel agency, who handled all Afzalia's travel, so we got top customer treatment from the management.

Here, we had to make arrangements with the studio. And, we had to be careful, for sometimes they screwed up the dates. Saeed the owner, was not always there but he had given me his office and home phone numbers. He was my Persian brother; I could call him at any time. Our three actors confirmed the dates through their assistants, but here the studio had given our dates to some other production.

Abba nervously told me, "Ali, call your friend Saeed." I got on the phone right away. In about an hour, he came. Firing his assistant, he said," Cancel the date of the other production, and give it to Movie Makers." Abba was so pleased and relieved, for it was his job to make sure that the studio was available. "And in the future," Saeed said, "if you make a mistake, don't wait for my orders. Just postpone the other production." I was happy with myself too, for I had started making connections already.

Zaffar picked up the actors from the airport in Sanlay bhaiya's car, and I accompanied him. Meena and Ejaz recognized me, and we led them to our car. I introduced Zaffar to Meena and Ejaz, and I said, "Himalya Sahab, I am Ali Reza, assistant to the production manager." He said, "How are you? I think you are my man." I was confused as I did not know what he meant.

We had the shoot the next morning, so we told them we would pick them up at ten and then left.

We arrived at the studios at around eleven, and the shooting started at 12 noon. By now, shooting had begun full swing. Even bhaiya had started staying on the sets; in fact, he, too, was in a couple of shots. Mazhar abba, I, and our helpers realized for the first time how difficult running a production house was; it was definitely not like a cozy desk job. We really had a big load on our shoulders, which we had least expected.

Apart from physical strain, we were bogged down in administrative details. But, at the same time, I was also thrilled at being a spoke in this giant wheel of the world of films. I was tough. Remember at the age of ten, my dad made me work in his restaurant till eleven p.m.? Well, that was standing in good stead now, for I could handle what was thrown at me.

Unlike today, recording the sound of actors' dialogues while being filmed was a tedious task in those days. The sound engineer would be on the set with his recording instruments. Just before the director said 'action', the sound engineer would start recording. This recorded sound tape had to be synchronized with the film while editing.

This time, the shoot lasted for two weeks, and when I dropped the actors to the airport, Himalay Walla pulled me aside and gave me his home phone number. "Ali", he said, "I need your help. You see, I have a lady here in Karachi who is my friend; and I come here and spent time with her.

Whenever I want to come to Karachi, I will call you in advance. You call me back the following day. My wife will answer the phone. Introduce yourself and tell her that I am wanted in Karachi for shooting. Make it sound urgent. If she asks you how long I am wanted for, just say it may be ten to fifteen days."

So, this is why he told me in our first meeting that I was his man. When I came home that night, I told Bhaiya about it. He smiled and shaking his head, he said, "Ali, welcome to the filmy world. I know about his affair. He knew he could trust you, which is why he asked for this favour, so please keep his secret." Naturally, I shared this with Mazhar Abba and Zaffar, but no one else.

After the shoot, I was very busy making sure that the editor was taken care of. This time, he had three reels of film to work with, which was a much longer task than before. I would sit with him and was learning how an editor works. Every day, I was becoming familiar with processes involved in making films. When the rushes were ready, Bhaiya invited a couple of the distributers, and Khizr invited some newspaper men. Charlie was there, too.

The idea was to give updates about the film to both the industry as well as the public interested in films. I had to make extra seating arrangements, for this time the crowd was much bigger. The lights were out, and the rushes started. It all looked great on the screen. I was proud that I was a part of what I was watching.

After that portion of the film was over, as usual, the guests congratulated everyone involved in its production, especially Bhaiya. Afzalia and

Sanlay bhaiya were very pleased, and they were the only ones to say to Mazhar Abba and me, "Thank you! We know you have worked hard." Hearing them say that felt great. In fact, Abba even said, "Ali worked harder than me."

Khizir gave the news reporters some still shots, which the still photographer had taken during the shoot. After the filming of each shot, the still photographer usually took the still shots, and it was Khizir who then gave it to the different men in different papers. There were different shots of Meena, Ejaz, Bhaiya, Hiamalaya and Charlie; all looked great: glossy black and white 8X10. These shots were later published in different entertainment newspapers.

I had started spending more and more time in the studios. During this time, I got to meet actors and actresses, like Allaudin, who was a tall, rugged man with a striking personality. He filmed mostly in Lahore, and by chance, had come to Karachi. I told him that my real name was Alladin while my nick name was Ali. He smiled and said, "We cannot have two Allaudins in the industry."

I briefly met Nigahat Sultana and Sabiha Khanum, and Santosh Kumar, her husband. They were nice enough to speak with me for about five minutes because I was with Movie Makers, which had become a big name in the industry by now. In our cheel walla bangala, where I lived with Bhaiya, we had an adjoining neighbour, Nizam. His sister-in-law was actress Nayyar Sultan, who was a delicate beauty. She was a good friend of ours.

Susie was coming to shoot for her film regularly with her mum on the sets. I, too, always joined them on the sets. By now some people had come to know of my close relationship with Susie. The director, sorry to say, was a very dark-skinned ugly, man who had an eye for Susie. He always tried in his vile, despicable way to make Susie, on the quiet of course, to go out with him. And then, on the other hand, was the camera man, who in his way, was trying the same.

That she would say yes was impossible, but Susie's fault was that because of her friendly nature, she never jilted them, and so they kept on hoping. Even the still photographer, who also did the stills for our movie, was in line. This was the way in films; everyone thought they had the right to pick up anyone they wanted. Now all these people knew about my love affair with Susie. Maybe they didn't know everything, but they knew that we both loved one another a lot.

So, one day, the still photographer, trying to curry favour with me, said, "Ali, if you allow me, I want to tell you something very important that no one knows. I have been debating with myself to tell you or not, but I decided I must. You know the director of Susie's film?" I said yes, and then he continued, "Well, my friends saw her at Hawks Bay alone with the director."

That night, I could not sleep. I told Zaffar what I had heard about Susie. "Ali," he said, "you know, they are all jealous of you, so they will say anything just to make you break up with her." He was asleep and I hoped he was right. It was not easy to just forget it. I could not sleep. I kept on assuring myself that she could not have done that.

Then the thought of how low girls stoop to get ahead in the films entered my mind. I kept on debating to and fro, and these thoughts were driving me crazy. I said to myself, 'I will call her to our place of rendezvous and slap the hell out of her.' I was going crazy and was starting to repent having fallen in love again. I had been enjoying my life, flirting with girls, and having Susie as my number one. There were no worries; I slept well. But then, I had to go and fall in love. It was past midnight and my teenage poetic mood took over.

To this world I like to say Thousand things by the way Don't fall in love, do anything Be happy, just dance and sing For if you fall in love today With worries your head will start to sway For trifle things you will say For heaven's sake, go away, go away No eat no drink, no peace no sleep Often like a kid you weep Can you explain this unique disease Which brings lovers to their feet The trouble with me, with all that speech I cannot practice what I preach.

As soon as Zaffar woke up the next morning, he glanced towards me and with his sleepy eyes, said, "Ali, don't tell me you did not sleep a wink last night. You are a fool. I promise you she will not do that to you. She loves you too much, and she is not that type of a girl." How I wish I had listened to him!

I called her and asked her to meet me after lunch. I walked across to our house and was waiting for her. My eyes were red with anger and the sleepless night I had had. As she entered, she said,

"Hi, Ali" and proceeded to kiss me. I pushed her aside and slapped her so hard on both her cheeks that I thought I had broken her jaw. She started crying, and in between, kept asking me what was the matter with me and why I had slapped her.

Then, I poured my heart out. I told her all that was pent up inside me since last night. I said all the bad things about girls like her, who would do any degrading thing to get ahead in the films. And I kept ranting all that came to my mind, no matter how bad. "Ali," she said, "I keep God as my witness, and swear on my mother's and fathers' life, if I have done this shameless thing then, oh God take them away. Ali, oh Ali how could you even think like this of me? How could you fall into the false gossip by such low people?" She was weeping, again. She said, "Ali, how could you level such false accusations?"

I was so mad at myself for believing that bastard still photographer, and for not believing Zaffar. He had said I am a fool, and fool I was for slapping this innocent gal of mine. I wanted to punish myself, so I picked up a small knife from the kitchen and slashed each of my forearm twice. It started bleeding. Scared, Susie brought a bowl of water, drenched two kitchen towels, and pressed hard on my wounds.

"Ali," she said, "I would been happy if you had just said you were sorry. Why did you have to hurt yourself like this?" She kept crying as she cooed me, "My darling, my love, my husband..." She tore two strips from her under skirt and bandaged my forearms. That was the first and the last time I ever raised my hand on a woman. I was ashamed of myself, first for not having faith in her and second, for being so damn fickle-minded and gullible.

"Susie," I said, "I am going to kill that bastard sill photographer." She tapped her forehead and said, "Ali, for Gods' sake, why do you want to create such problems? The newspapers will have a field day with our story.

Please Ali, swear on my life, you will not do anything. Just pretend that you never believed him the first place." Before she left that day, she took my hand and placed it on her head and said, "Swear on my life that you will never believe these people again. You know I go to shootings with my mum. AND NEVER ALONE."

That evening, Zaffar, Musti, and I went to the nightclub. With the shootings and other production-related things, I anyway didn't get as many chances to go out as before. While drinking, I said, "Zaffar, I wish I had listened to you about Susie's innocence." At this point, Musti interrupted me and asked what I was talking about. I told him the whole story, and he, too, said the same thing as Zaffar, and added that he had known Susie since their school days, and nobody had ever said anything bad about her.

I continued with my foolishness, and told them about slapping her, and all that had transpired after that. I showed them my forearm, still bandaged. Anyway, all is well that ends well. And, my love for Susie increased by ten folds. I promised myself that I will make sure that she never has to go through such stupidity of mine again, and that she is never unhappy. Musti dropped us home, and that night I slept like a baby.

The next morning, Zaffar even dropped the kids to school, which he rarely did. He was a real brother to me. As usual, Mazhar abba came to know of what was happening. "Ali," he said, "I know all that is going on in your life, and beta, do not rush to form judgment on anything." Between shootings, rush prints, and buying raw materials, there used to be some free time sometimes that I spent in Maritime with my dearest Hamid mamoo and the staff. In order to not disrupt their work, we used to go down to the canteen for lunch - usually Zaffar, Hamid mamoo, and myself.

Hamid Mamoo used to say, "Ali, tell me all that has been going on in the studios, your love life, and everything else." I always kept him informed, for he was my genuine well-wisher, and like Mazhar abba, also my guide. It felt nice that I had these people in my life.

Saeed Haroon called one morning at around eleven. Bhaiya spoke to him. "Shaida Sahab," he said, urgency in his voice, "Can you please send Ali to the studios immediately? I have some German guests, and I want him to be their guide for the day, as I am too busy." I arrived at the studios and went to Saeeds' office. And there, sitting, having cold drinks were husband, wife, and their daughter, who was a smashing beauty. "This is Captain Godtmann, his wife, and Lorlouise, his daughter," Saeed introduced. I shook hands with them but could not get my eyes off Lorlouise.

I said, "Captain, I will first give you a tour of the studios and show you shooting of a film. Then, we can go shopping or whatever else you guys desire." We started from the hall, where we tried our rush prints. And then, I took them to the sets where Shamim Ara was shooting Kunwari Beywa. It was her first film, and the great director Naqui was directing her. We sat behind the cameraman, and next to the sound engineer.

After the shot, I introduced the Captain and his family first to Naqui sahab, then to my new friend Shamim Ara, and the sound engineer. After introductions, I took them to our office and Shamim joined us, too. I could see the Godtmann family were very happy and pleased with the experience. Clearly, Lorlouise was excited. Then, we went shopping to Bori Bazaar, where they bought a few souvenirs. I could see Lorlouise was interested in me, as I was in her.

They were tired, and so, took their leave to go back to the ship. The studio car dropped them to the ship, and the captain said, "Ali, can we get lunch tomorrow and then catch a movie for Lorlouis loves movies?" I said, "Well, of course!" He further added, "Can you come to the ship? We will have some beer, and then go to Karachi for the day."

The moment the film started, without wasting any time, I brushed my hand on hers and she held my hand tight. The moment she took my hand, a warm electrical current took over my entire body. Am I lucky or am I lucky, I thought. After the movies, we went back to the ship where Lorelouise and her mother went to their cabins to freshen up. And I had a beer, and the captain had a peg of Johnny Walker Black Label. Then, we freshened up and all sat down for dinner. The table was laid out by the steward, and there were prawns, steaks, salads, and dark German bread.

Once a year, the captain was allowed to take his family on the ship for a whole journey. Of course, on the ship, he received a royal treatment. After we finished, the captain said to Lorelouise in German, "You can take him to your cabin." That is how their culture was; he did not have any problem with us teenagers spending time together. She held my hand and took me to her cabin. Once we were in her cabin, she put on a slow music, and we were cuddling, necking, and smooching. And that is all.

We were lost in the ecstasy of the moment. The next day was their last day there, for the ship had off-loaded and loaded all her cargo. One more night of the same with Lorlouise, and then it would be time for farewell, and to say goodbye. She gave me her address to write to her, followed a last long-lasting kiss. The captain and his wife thanked me for giving them a wonderful time. What is goodbye and separation but a wave, a tear and a smile?

I was really sad that Lorlouise had gone. I missed her very much, and she also missed me for she mailed a letter to me from the next port. I did not reply for I was waiting for her return to Bremen. And then I would write. I still have her address, it's in my diary. Maritime always printed some notebooks in hard copy to distribute to our shipping clients. I still have one. Now, I was receiving letters from Sydney and Germany, which kept their memories alive.

Our film's shoot was progressing, and Bhaiya asked Mazhar abba to scout for a desert location outside Karachi. Abba and I set out driving in the direction we were given. It took us two hours to finally locate a very suitable location: all sand with palm trees spread out. It was just perfect. The next day, we took Bhaiya and Gilani to the location, and both of them said, "Good job you two."

Charlie, the director in the film within our film, was to direct Rakshi's gypsy dance, and the shooting day was fixed. On the day of shooting, Nizam Bhai, our neighbour wanted to come, so Rakshi and Afzal the cameraman came with him. In our van, I took all lighting equipment, the boys, reflectors, etc. The drive was about forty-five minutes. Abba brought Bhaiya, Charlie, and Gilani to the location. In between shots I, whisked Rakshi away from the crowd and laying on the sand, we caressed and kissed. I just cannot help it; I was born this way. I could never stay away from pretty girls.

I continued to grapple with my resolve to love Susie and get married to her. We took many pictures with Charlie, Gilani, and Mazhar abba. These pictures became some very beautiful memories. I have them in my cherished collection. We packed up at sunset, and the gypsy dance sequence was completed to the satisfaction of Moheb and Gilani. Soon after the shooting, one evening, Bhaiya, in the presence of our family, said, "Ali, Mazhar is going to Africa to get married. So, from now on, you will be the acting Production Manager. Mazhar has assured me that you can handle everything on your own, and knowing you, I am confident you will."

Smiling, I said, "Bhaiya, I promise I will not let you down. By the grace of Allah, I am now familiar with all aspects of this job, and then you are also here to guide me, so I have no worries at all." That night, as usual, I thanked God after my prayers for giving me a loving family, and above all, my film world. My work had doubled over night; it was really tough, but I was not complaining. Once again, the shooting started in full swing and Meena, Ejaz, and Himalaya Walla came on a long trip. This time, the shoot schedule was at least twenty-five days long. Zaffar helped in picking up the artists from the airport. He would have loved to do more, but he had his Maritime job.

One Saturday evening, a grand party was arranged at Le Gourmet, the famous night club. Afzalia took care of the whole shebang. The creme of the society was here, including our filmy people. Meena had come with her friend, a healthy, wealthy, and attractive guy from Lahore. The best of drinks and food was served, and this time all the expenses were born by Movie Makers. It was a memorable night. The party ended at around three a.m. for by then everyone had gone home.

Bhaiya was so proud that his party was such a success. He was the most important figure there, and I was happy for him. As they say, no rest for the wicked, so, although it was Sunday, I rushed to the studios after breakfast to arrange for the rushes. The shooting resumed from Monday. And I was running around like a chicken with its head cut off. I was overwhelmed, but I was managing it without a flaw. This shooting schedule was over within twenty-one days, and we bagged a few more reels.

The following week was the D-day when I would be shooting with Charlie. Bhaiya gave me a two-page script and explained in detail what the scene entailed. I was to portray a nervous kid approaching a director - Charlie - to get a chance to act in the Gilani films. And then, there was some dialogue between the two. It reminded me of the time in Bombay when, at the age of ten, I had approached the director, Jagdish Sethi. 'Then, I was not nervous at all, so why would I be nervous now', I kept reassuring myself.

But then I thought I was not facing the camera then, but now I would be. And then, there was the formidable Charlie, who was not generous with his fellow actors once the camera was on. On the day of the shooting, I sat in the make-up room, and the make-up artist said," Ali, you just need some light make up, for you have good, fair complexion." Bhaiya was so worried that he kept on assuring me to the last moment, even in the make-up room. I loved him for that. I stepped on the set; I was tad more nervous than I had anticipated. Moheb took me by my hand and said, "Ali, listen carefully... This is your mark, and this is the field in which you can move.

But you have to remain within the field otherwise you will be out of the camera range."

Charlie was sitting on the desk, not on his chair. He was a creative actor. Chikoo (also her first shot and film), a teenage girl was standing next to his desk, as his secretary. I was taking in all that, while Moheb was guiding me. Meanwhile, Gilani was instructing the light men to spot the light on all the actors with different lights. From my days in school plays, I had trained myself how to focus and get rid of nervousness. Behind curtains, before stepping on the stage, I would close my eyes for a minute, and only concentrate on the play. And then, I would be ready.

Waiting for the word 'action' from the director, I was ready to make my mark in acting. Lights - Silence — Action. I started walking towards Charlie slowly, as I was next to the desk. He got up went around - not in the script - but then that is the way he was - did not bother me, I waited for him to sit back on the desk, and after he said his dialogue, I enacted my role without a flaw, and gave a perfect shot in only one take, although my dialogues was two minutes long.

Moheb said 'cut', and Charlie was actually the first one to pick me up in his arms and congratulate me! Bhaiya was so happy that he hugged me and said, "Ali, I knew you could do it." Gilani, camera man Afzal, and everyone else were also full of praise. Charlie later told me, "Ali, many actors have to give many takes when shooting with me, but you did it in one take." Our director Moheb said, "Ali, tell you the truth, I thought that we would have to shoot many takes before you could get it right, as we have to do with the newcomers. But you gave me a pleasant surprise, and I am proud of you. Now start rehearsing with Rakshi for the big shoot of your rock and roll dance. I want you to get her ready."

That night, at the dinner table, Bhaiya said, "Ali was just fantastic! He acted very naturally and nailed it in the first take." Bhabhi said with a smile, "So, we now have one more actor in the family." The next morning, I rushed to the studios. There was a big load now for the editor and his assistant to get the rushes ready. First, we had to work on the few reels we had shot of Meena, followed by the others that would take many days. And then, my shot. I was impatient, and kept asking the editor, Iqbal when he would start working on my shot. He laughed and said, "Ali yaar, you have to wait. We will do yours soon." My excitement was only natural as it was my first time, and I wanted to see myself in action on the small editing screen.

After a week, Iqbal worked on my rushes, and for the first time I saw myself on the small screen. I was overjoyed and exuberant! I could not express it in words, and Iqbal said, "Ali, you were very good." I said to myself, l think I can act. About five reels of rushes were ready for viewing, but Afzalia asked Bhaiya to postpone it for a couple of days. He further added that Shiro Kido, the biggest Japanese film producer would be arriving soon. So, we could all see the rushes with him. The mains of the shipping company, who were friends of Mr. Kido, had called from Japan and told Afzalia of his visit to Karachi.

Bhaiya said, "Ali, you should also invite Susie to come. She will get a chance to meet Mr. Kido." It was so thoughtful of him, for whenever he could, he would include her in the family. Once, all the Imams had planned a dinner at Le Gourmet. Susie was also invited, and Bhaiya made sure she sat between him and Bhabhi, to further establish her as part of the family. I would have given my life for Bhaiya any day.

The prints were great and looked beautiful on the screen. Oh boy! I was so thrilled to see myself on a movie theatre screen for the first time. I was so happy that I hugged Zaffar, who was sitting next to me. Shiro Kido looked very pleased, and some pictures were taken of him in our auditorium.

After viewing the rushes, we all went for a late lunch to our house. A tasty meal was cooked as usual by the Bihari cook, arranged by Sanlay bhaiya had arranged. Rakshi, Susie, and others were not invited, for this was a private party.

Bhaiya had asked me to make sure that I served Mr. Kido all the dishes so he would taste every food on the table. It was a buffet lunch, and everyone filled their plates and stood aside for eating. I first served Mr. Kido, and then myself. As usual, the food was out of this world, and my fav Bihari kabab, was always part of the menu. Mr. Kido was all praises for the lunch. He said he had tasted all kinds of foods on his world trip, and this one was the best. Sanlay bhaiya had instructed the cook to make it medium hot, so as to make it easy on Mr. Kido's stomach.

Another lunch party was arranged the next day for Mr. Kido. I had sent a ticket for Ejaz to come from Lahore. The party was in Le Gourmet, and that too, was a great success. Ejaz was introduced as our hero of the film. The next day, Mr. Kido left. He promised Bhaiya that if at all there was a possibility of a joint venture, he would inform him. Musti was a regular in all our parties. He always helped with his car when we needed help for our shootings, or other tasks. He was a real pal; he also drove our artists, and we got all the help we needed.

Mazahar abba was back with his wife Nayyar before Mr. Kido's visit. When they both first came, she was welcomed by all the Imams, and Abba looking at me, said, "Nayyar, this is my son." She smiled at me, and said, "So, I am your amma." Movie Makers was now established as the biggest producers of Pakistan so far. Hence when a German Film Production company (the name of which now escapes me, I think it was something like ARCA Production) came, they wanted to meet Movie Makers.

They had worked on a storyline depicting the time of the Partition. It was titled the Journey to Pakistan. Afzalia also had shipping connections in Hamburg, and the production company were from Hamburg. As Mr. Kido was introduced to him, so was this Germany company. Afzalia invited them, and at the airport Afzalia and Bhaiya met them. The following day, a big meeting was set between them, Bhaiya, Sanlay bhaiya, and Afzalia. After two days of discussions, the Germans left, after giving Bhaiya two copies of the script.

The agreement was that it would be a joint venture between them and Movie Makers, with fifty-percent share in profits and expenses for each. The movie was to be made in two languages, English and Urdu, which entailed two shots of each scene. Once the actors would say the dialogues in English, and then once in Urdu. This would take at least two years to produce, but it was a venture we were prepared to embark on.

One night after dinner, Bhaiya sat with me in his room, and narrated the story to me. He said, "Ali, we are starting a very big movie, the likes of which Pakistan has not seen." After he gave me the gist of the story, he said, "We are planning to take Neelo as the heroine, and a newcomer for the role of hero. And Ali, you will be one of the lead support." And, I could hear my heart beating hard against my chest. Me? Lead support? And he continued, "The actual lead actor of the film will be Charles Boyer, the very famous French - American actor. The German producers have already signed an agreement with him."

1947 was the year of the partition. Around fifteen million Muslims and Hindus set on a journey, which was mostly on foot. And, some made the journey on trains and buses. Hindus were going to India, and Muslims were going to Pakistan. Young, old, healthy, sick... all had to find the courage to embark on this impossible journey. Bhaiya explained, "The role of the priest is to comfort the old and the sick, and would also be involved in family dramas, like Neelo's romance with her beau. According to his teachings, he would try to heal with kind words and God's blessings, for medical supplies were scarce."

He continued, "This is a gist of his role, but he and you will carry the film.

And now your role - you are a young, poor boy who was surviving on the streets of Bombay with your monkey. You used to do madari ka khel, meaning in Indian performing on the street with a monkey doing different tricks. You are clad in torn, dirty shirt, and a fungi - which is a cloth tied around your waist. This way, you are entertaining people when they take a brake to rest from this tedious journey. You would walk with the priest and help him when he is comforting people. It's all about human endurance, and faith", Bhaiya concluded.

He then said, "I have just given you an abbreviated version of a very long film, and I must say, Ali, you are very lucky this has come your way. When this film is completed, you will get exposure in Europe and America."

I rushed towards him, took him behind the shack, and asked him to give me, just for fifteen minutes, his torn upper garment, the stick he was carrying, and the monkey to go with it. In turn, I would give him two rupees. He agreed; I removed my shirt and wore his. It took me a couple of minutes to become friendly with the monkey. I asked that madari chap to stay out of sight, and I walked in front of the porch where everyone was seated and was having lunch. I kept on calling madari ka khel - meaning monkey tricks - everyone was busy talking and eating, they did not notice.

But, the first one to notice me was Zaffar. In his excitement, he kept calling, "This is Ali." All got up and started laughing; and I made the monkey do some tricks, like a summer salt. Bhaiya said, "Ali, you have proved you are ready for our new venture." Sanlay bhaiya said, "Ali sach- mooch kamaal karta Koi (meaning he really does wonders)..." I still have this picture in my treasure cove of photos. Zaffar said, "Ali, take a dip in the sea to get the filth off from the madari's clothes." But, I told him in acting we must be prepared to make all sacrifices. On our return, everyone was talking about my creativity.

A big shoot day was ahead of us. Himalaya Walla had arrived from Lahore, and the whole crew was asked to assemble. Zaffar was also to take part in the scene but playing double for Bhaiya.

According to the plot, the villain is trying to escape from the crime scene in which Meena is involved. He jumps in a car, speeding away, and Bhaiya is chasing him in our old Jaguar. We drove around the roads where the final shoot would take place, and after a couple of rehearsals, we were ready to shoot. Zaffar was behind the Jaguars' wheel, the back of his head looked more like Bhaiya's, and that is why he doubled for him, who did not know how to drive.

Afzal the cameraman and I sat back in the jaguar. He had set the camera for high-speed chase, and I was helping him with the accessories. Zaffar alone in the front was driving at a very high speed, chasing the car in front. He was a very good driver, and I had total faith in him. It was windy, and all of a sudden, the hood of the jaguar got loose and opened fully on its hinges. Zaffar could not see anything, for the hood was blocking all view in the front. Afzal said, "Zaffar, stop before we get into an accident."

Zaffar was not about to stop; he said, "Afzal, keep on shooting, I know there is no traffic in front, and this is a good shot. It will bring a good effect on the screen." We are driving in an adversely dangerous situation just to catch the villain. I was not afraid at all, but Afzal... I could see his face; the poor chap was sweating with fear. He kept shooting and pleading for Zaffar to stop. Finally, Zaffar stopped, and then there was a cut-to-cut shot showing Bhaiya coming out of the Jaguar, and wrestling with the villain and overcoming him.

All this time Bhaiya had been following us in another car. He, too, was on pins and needles. He was very worried. "Zaffar", he said, "this was a very dangerous stunt you pulled. We are lucky nothing happened." Zaffar said, "Bhaiya, if I was not confident, I would have stopped." We tied the hood down with a string and drove back home. Zaffar asked me, "Ali, I could feel you were not scared, and you were encouraging Afzal to keep on. I knew you are brave." I simply replied, "Of course. After all, you taught me how to drive."

Surprisingly, this time Himalaya Walla had come to Karachi with his wife.

Sanlay bhaiya

arranged a dinner party at his house. Among the guests were Himalaya Walla, Mr. Watanabe, his partner from Japanese shipping, and us. Once again, we were in for a treat of Bihari cooking, which never failed to give pleasure to our palates. As always, pictures were taken, which the Japanese loved to take home for their families. It was my hobby too. I have been collecting pictures from the time I was six. I have the original prints of all these photos, and I tell you they make great memories. Today, as I am writing this, the children and grandchildren of the Imam families have seen these pictures.

The rushes of the chase scene and the fight sequence were ready. Himalaya Walla brought his wife to join all of us for the viewing. As usual, our prints came out great, and when the scene of the Jaguar's hood came, everybody in the auditorium, cried out 'wow'. After the rushes, everyone congratulated Zaffar for this dare devil act.

Himalaya Walla said, "Zaffar, you have really put a lot of spice in this shot." Cameraman Afzal said, "Zaffar, you scared the hell out of me, but it was worth the scare."

Twice a week, I was trying to get Rakshi to learn the rock and roll steps, but she could not get it. She did the jive, and that in itself was not enough. It was tough for she was double boned and heavy. She was not flexible, which is important in doing all the acrobats in the dance. After days of breaking my back, she only could do one step, which involved her running towards me and throwing herself at me with her legs spread. I was supposed to catch her by her waist and lift her up only to throw her back on the floor on her feet. And then, we would continue to dance.

I did not discourage her, I told her she was ready, and that we would meet on the day of our shoot. Moheb asked me if she was ready, I explained to him in detail. And he said, "Okay, you take care of it for I, too, have not filmed a rock roll dance." The shoot date was set after a week. Meanwhile Rushdi, our playback singer was practicing the song. The lyrics - Nach Ley, Nach Nach — were written by Khizir with Khurshid copying the music from Rock Around the Clock. It was not bad and had the beat, but they could not record it in time for our shoot, so the filming was postponed.

During my last days in Maritime, before Movie Makers, a new employee by the name of Sultan, joined the agency as a shipping clerk. His father, who had some important position in the port, had used his influence with Afzalia to secure the job for his son. Sultan was known as Soli and was a big guy with a crew cut and glasses which made him look unfriendly. But, once you got to know him, he was the best funny friend to have around. Zaffar and I became good friends with him, and sometimes went to dine and dance. He used to smoke a big cigar whenever he was out of the office and had some funny ways about him.

In one instance, we had gone to Metropole Hotel to dine. We had been sitting for hardly five minutes, and Soli was impatient. "Why is the waiter not coming", he said, and in the next instance, picked up the plate on which the serviette was, held it high and said, "See how the waiter will rush to our table now". He let go the plate, which fell on the floor and broke to pieces. The waiter came running, and all heads were turned towards us. Soli casually made a gesture with his hand towards other diners, meaning all is okay. This is the way he was. We were embarrassed, but amused. Zaffar said, "Soli, promise that you would have no more such outbursts", and he only had a sheepish grin to offer as a response.

The Karachi film industry, unfortunately, did not have financiers to support the good directors who had really good stories to film. The only finance which came in was venture capital, but that, too, was not enough to sustain for five or six reels of shoot. I was acting in three such films, two untitled and one stunt film by the name of Black Queen. In the latter, I was the brother of the heroine, with my love interest who was a newspaper reporter. She too was from Bombay, where she did supporting roles.

In one film, Yvonne, Susie's first cousin and a good dancer was opposite me. She had never been in the films, and did not want to, but had agreed to this one on my request. I wish she was my dancing partner in Sitaron Ki Duniya; she was light and prettier than Rakshi. She easily picked up all the acrobatic rhythm that I had taught her. Compared to her, the only thing which Rakshi had going for her was that she was well-known in films.

All three films were canned only after a few reels because of lack of funds. The rushes of these films were great; financiers used to be invited to view these reels. They liked it but were reluctant to risk their money. By now, Rushdi had recorded the rock-and-roll song, and the date was set for the shoot. Moheb, Gilani, and I went to Le Gourmet to make all arrangements for the shooting. I had to show them the field I needed to move around, without going out of the camera range.

Zaffar had some friends who I was meeting for the first time, like Haider, an air force pilot who was as tough as they come. Then, there was his friend, a Sindhi Vaderah, whose name escapes me. Sindhi Vadera had a mistress: a pretty, young Irish girl whose name was Ann. She was introduced to me. We were all at the bar, drinking. Lights, Silence, Action - the dance started, the band on the stage started to play in a mock way, for we were actually dancing to our own song Nachle, Nachle. There were a couple of foreigner girls dancing with their partners in the background, and I did what I was good at.

By 5 PM, Moheb said, "Pack up" because the night club had to re arrange all the tables and chairs for their own night guests. I was not satisfied with the shoot, because it was planned that we will shoot the whole sequence with the camera placed for a mid-shot range. After that, I wanted close up shots for different steps, especially a very close-up shot of my fast-moving feet, which would be added in editing. Well, there was no time and we could not afford to rent another day.

The dance rushes were completed and ready for viewing. Afzalia made it a point to come, for he had come to our shoot, Himalaya Walla was there, too. Zaffar Khursheed, the music director; Rushdi the singer, and the crew were all there. I was really very nervous, Bhaiya and Bhabi said, "Don't worry, Ali. It will be fine." The film began, and to my surprise, it was filmed very well and looked absolutely great, especially the shot where I come running and jumping over the table, and land on my knees and ankles simultaneously on the floor where Rakshi was waiting for me.

Yes, it was good. Everyone was full of praise and congrats. They all said, "This dance, for sure, will be one of the highlights of the film." Himalaya Walla said, "Ali, I had not seen a rock-and-roll dance, and this was great and an exhilarating experience for me." This was the first time in my life that I felt it was the biggest accolade I ever received. It made me so happy that I thought I would burst. Bhaiya should take all the credit; he was the writer of the story, and in its original script there was no such character like mine.

But when he saw and heard all the time of my dancing championships, he created a role for me in the picture. Thank God he did. I wrote to my sister, Meher the next day, and she wrote back, "We are all proud of you!" My youngest brother Farrokh was already following on my footsteps, and Mum kept asking, with tears in her eyes when I would be visiting her, and I used to have tears when I used to read their letter. As I am writing this, I have moist eyes.

I had not forgotten Munna and Amma, for I never could forget my first home in Karachi. So, I visited them when I had the time. On two such occasions, when I was going back home after mu lunch with them, I saw Nusrat in a car with her mother. It was evident that they had gone shopping in Bori Bazaar. We had stopped at a traffic signal; I was in the van, and since our van was higher than their car, I had a clear view below. She was sitting with some bags on her lap, and no smile or happiness on her face.

What was I to think? I thought she was not happy, but I dismissed that thought by convincing myself that perhaps she was tired after shopping. But as God is my witness, the second time I saw her, it was with the same sad look on her face. After the second time, seeing her like that, I, too became sad. My sadness intensified when I saw hearse carrying a coffin, with two cars following with flower wreaths. An uncomfortable and eerie feeling took over me, that night at home, I related it to Zaffar and told him I was feeling inspired to write a poem.

Zaffar was fast asleep, when I started penning my inspiration in a poem. The wreaths I had seen that day inspired me to write on flowers:

FLOWERS, FLOWERS, FLOWERS OH THESE
LOVELY FLOWERS UPON THIS GREEN EARTH

ENDOWED WITH DIFFERENT POWERS

LOVER OFFERS TO HIS LADY FAIR

IN FORGIVENESS FLOWERS DO THEIR SHARE

YELLOW AND GREEN GOLDEN AND WHITE
HAPPINESS OR SORROW AT ITS SIGHT

EVENTS OF WEDDING GARLANDS TAKE

THE PLACE OF WREATH THE FLOWERS MAKE
TOMBSTONES LOOK SO FULL OF GLOOM

ELATED THE BRIDAL SUITE FULL OF BLOOM

After breakfast I showed it to Zaffar, and he said, "Ali turn sach mooch shayar ho" - meaning 'you are really a poet'.

Now about Ann, the Sindhi Vaderah's mistress: she had lost her parents and did not have the wherewithal to survive, for her parents had died penny-less. Being very attractive, she was spotted by Vaderah (Sindhi landlords) shortly after — and he looked after her. I had met her before I was introduced to the Vaderah, on the day of my rock-and-roll shoot, and we had gotten very close and had been meeting secretly. One of Zaffar S good friends was Rana, a real tough guy with a good personality; he had few people under him. He was kind of a don. Rana was also a friend of the Vaderah, and when he came to know about my affair, he called Zaffar and asked him to meet him as there was a matter of utmost importance.

Rana knew me too, but he wanted to speak to Zaffar first, and he told him, "Zaffar, Ali is playing a dangerous game. He is having an affair with Anna." He further added, "I came to know through my people, and if the Vaderah comes to know, he will arrange for Ali to vanish. I have stopped this in its track, tell Ali to stop immediately, for I, too will not be able to help." Zaffar was scared for me, for he knew how dangerous those people could be, and asked me to stop it right then. It was a short affair, but great while it lasted. Later I found out that she had contracted leukemia.

Even all these affairs did not make me falter in my love for Susie. I have been steadfast and constant with my love for her, for we had decided to get married. She was going on a trip to Bombay with sister Deborah and had asked me to intimate my sister of her visit. I wrote to Meher about it. They were all anxiously waiting to receive her, especially my mum. She wanted to be sure that I am getting married to the right person.

Much before Susie's visit to Bombay, I told her I would marry her if she agrees to two of my conditions. The first condition was that she would have to leave the film industry. The second condition was that she would have to become a Muslim. I didn't have a problem with her being Jewish. In fact, I used to even sing their hymns with them. But when we would have children, they would struggle with two identities, and I didn't want that for her. She agreed and kept her word. When new films came, she refused. Her parents were angry, for her films were an added source of income. Deborah did not show any opposition, and Eddie, he loved me like his brother, and I him. He was all for it.

Susie had her cousin living in Bandra, Bombay, and on their arrival, they received them, and arranged for their tour etc. It included a visit to the film studios. Mehboob Productions were filming Mother India with the great inimitable Nargis and the not-so-famous actor of that time, Sunil Dutt.

Susie and family visited the outdoor shooting of the film where Susie was introduced to Nargis and Sunil as the heroine of about 10 films in Karachi. They welcomed her and took some pictures, which I still have. The film went on to become a classic, and to date it's considered as one of the greatest classics of the Indian film Industry.

Susie then went to see my mother, sisters, and my brothers Farrokh and Saifu. It's not easy to not like Susie, but she had harboured within her a great fear that my mum might not accept her. As soon as she entered our house, she started hugging everybody, and they fell in love with her. I knew she knew how to win hearts. My mum was sick and in bed, and Susie did not waste time; she started feeding her in bed and pampering her. My mum, too, loved her the very moment she had stepped in our house. Susie sat next to her in bed, and said, "Mummy, you know I want to get married to Ali. Please give us your blessings." I knew my mum would put the same conditions to her, and Susie assured my mum she already had met with the conditions. My mum kissed her on each cheek and gave her blessings.

Upon Susie's return, we met at our love nest, and I was happy to welcome her back, I had really missed her. She told me how wonderful my family was and how they had given her the royal treatment. She loved all but her two favourites were my sister Meher and my brother Farrokh. She said my brother told her that he was following my footsteps. "Ali", she said "your mum thinks of you all the time, and she kept on asking me, with tears in her eyes, when you would be going to Bombay. Seriously Ali, you should take a trip, I could see her eyes are just pining to see you." I told Susie, "I am so busy with the film right now. As soon as it gets completed, God willing I will visit mother."

She bought with her a beautiful still, and it inspired me, and I wrote this acrostic poem, in our lovers' nest.

Steadily kindles the flame of love Unique is the ways of heaven above Sometimes joy and sometimes woe In love, God blessings bestow Exquisite is HIS grace.

Our film was nearing completion. Only a few scenes were left for shoot, which we completed in a month, and the toughest, time exhausting work would now start — Editing. If certain shots needed a reshoot, then again, we'd have to do the same rigmarole. And, getting a date from the censor board to get their approval was another thing. They were slow, and to get a date from them was another tedious procedure. We applied and we got a date for two months ahead. That would have been enough time for us, provided nothing went wrong.

In film production I had learnt one thing: one should not be under the false impression that everything would fall into place in time. It was just not feasible. We had to do two re-shoots of Meena for a song sequence, and with a small crew. I had to take the place of the Clapman. I was like a joker, tried to fit in everywhere. Editing would start at ten in the morning and lasted up to three or four a.m. Bhaiya, Moheb the editor, and his assistant would all be involved. Bhaiya would help the whole day, and then I used to take him home. Then, I would come back to the studios to help out with whatever they needed.

First and foremost, all the positive prints, which were roughly fifteen reels, were edited and ready to view as a complete film in our studio auditorium. Bhaiya, Moheb, Gilani, and the sound engineer, along with our family, watched it. Then, the four of them came to an agreement that a scene had to be cut as it did not have much to do with the story. Now, the final editing of the negatives, with sound home synchronizing, was the most difficult task. This would take a long time, and we were worried that we would miss the censorship date.

So, we started working round the clock, and at this stage only the editors and I were working, with little breaks for tea and snacks. The kitchen was working along with us, making tea all the time. It was mostly caffeine which kept us going. I slept on our office couch; the editors also slept a wink or two, and then continued with the work. Although they were young, it was still taking its toll. But it had to be done; there was no way out, for if we missed the date, it would take at least two months for the next date.

The editors and I - we broke our backs, burning the candle at both ends to meet the deadline. At this stage, I have no problem saying that the editors and I put the most labour of love in the production of the film. No doubt Bhaiya had put many hours into writing the script, but he did that anyway even before the project of the film came up. We were now approaching the censorship date. Nearly two consecutive months had gone by, and my routine was to go home in the morning, take a shower, change my smelly clothes, and rush back. In the mornings Bhaiya accompanied me to the studio, assured the editors of bonus, even before the film was released. Of course, I was not offered; Bhaiya would want that, but Sanlay bhoiyo would not, so Bhaiya never asked him. After all I was part of the family, and I did not feel bad or expect anything.

Hurrah! One week before the deadline, we achieved the impossible! Bhaiya was so grateful that he hugged me and said, "Ali, I am thankful! You have made all of us proud." I said "Bhaiya, it was tough, but it was our home project, and I would have done anything to help. I am thankful to you... that you saw in me the makings of a good film manager."

Mazhar Abba and I delivered the film to the Censor Board, and we were informed that it might take about fifteen days for the certificate.

Meanwhile, Khizir was contacting the cinema houses where the film would be shown. The main cinema house was Light House on Bunder Road. In those days, posters for films were done by artists, using canvas and oil paint. We had the best one in Karachi, who was very good in his art. Bhaiya gave the still shot of Rakshi and me in the great pose, where I am holding her by the waist, her legs side of my hips. This poster was six-feet-long and five-feet-wide. This would be hung right above the entrance of Light House. On each side would be four-feet wide and three-feet high posters of Meena and Ejaz and Charlie and Bhaiya.

On the day of premiere, the press, the prospective distributors, our film crew, actor Charlie, some guests of the Imams, and the Imam families came to see the film. Susie was also invited, for she had appeared as a guest artist in our film: she as the Maharani, Bhaiya as the Maharaja, and I, as the Prime Minister. Barde Ghulamali sings a classic dhun. In a scene where Bhaiya was wrestling and fighting with the villain, little Shakil was yelling on top of his voice, "Hit him, daddy! Hit him, daddy!" And the crowd roared in laughter. Everybody loved the film, and we got good reviews in the end. Now, it was left for the public to either make or break our two years' hard work.

The first week, we had all theatres packed. In the second week, the rush gradually slowed down. I would always check the halls' attendance after the film started. I had started feeling sad and disappointed that the movie had failed at the box office. Reports from Lahore were the same; it was discouraging and disheartening. Everyone who was involved in making this film was puzzled and perplexed. They could not understand what had happened. The movie had the best of actors, directors and crew. How the movie had failed was beyond everyone's understanding. When all was said and done, Sanlay Bhaiya and the accountant declared a total loss of five lakhs. This was unheard of in Pakinstani films, for no other production company had ever ventured to put so much in one film.

In hindsight, we all agreed that the film was way ahead of its time; a film story within a film was too much for the mass audience to understand. If the same film were produced today, with all the modern techniques, it would be a success. The movie involved the highest paid actors, lavish parties in night clubs to entertain friends and introduce the actors, and it also involved the frequent visits of Mr. Kido and other German producers. All costs were borne by Movie Makers, and sadly, they could not be recovered. One top producer from Lahore later told Bhaiya, that he could produce three films in that big budget.

The following day, Movie Makers was dissolved, and the only employee was me. Sanlay Bhaiya called me in his office, gave me a month's salary, and said, "Ali, I am sorry. There's no Movie Makers anymore so you don't have a job." I put my head down, thanked him, and went home in a rickshaw. I was very disappointed with him. How could he do this to me, I could not stop thinking. I was the lowest paid employee whose salary was a paltry sum of 180 rupees monthly. This would not have made any dent in their holdings, for sure.

He could have given me my Maritime job back. But he was so angry with this whole movie making business. The only one he could vent his anger out was poor me. Bhaiya told me, "Ali, you know I had no say in the matter. As a matter of fact, I, too, have lost my perks. I will only be getting enough to keep his house running. You know you will continue staying here like before, and you will always be my son." Bhabhi, too, said, "I cannot understand how Wali Imam did this to this poor hardworking boy."

I did not stop loving Sanlay bhaiya. It was just that I was very heart broken. At that moment, I felt that unlike all the other Imams, he did not consider me as a family member. And, that hurt me more. The next morning, I was still in shock, and just could not think straight. I called Susie and told her to meet me at our love nest immediately. She said, "Ali, darling is everything okay? You don't sound your usual self." I told her I would explain later.

After that blow, it felt great to be in her arms. I narrated to her the whole heartbreaking situation. While caressing me, she said, "Ali you have always said that Allah looks out for you, and that if one door closes, HE opens another one for you. Trust that HE knows the best for you." That made me feel myself again and I was not brooding any more. All of a sudden, I said to Susie, "My darling, you have opened my eyes. I do not see any prospect here; I am going to my country Iran. Remember I used to teach those girls rock and roll? I used to see all the fashionable magazines... even at that time I knew that one day I would go to Teheran." Her first reaction was - What?

And she started crying, it was my turn now, to console her. "Look", I said, "your mum will never agree to our marriage, right?" She nodded, so I told her, "First, I will be going to Bombay to see my family and from there I will go to Iran." She asked, "What will happen to me?" I assured her that one day before I leave, we would get married. I told her that I would send for her once I reached Teheran. "I will give you the details later. The first thing I have to do is go to Javed, my Iranian's friend's house. Since he works at the Iranian Embassy, he will be able to give me some guidance."

She was still crying, but she had calmed down slightly. That night at dinner, Bhaiya told me that Afzalia had called and asked to tell me that he would arrange whatever help I needed. I said, "Bhaiya, I see no prospects in working in Karachi. I am planning to go to Teheran via Bombay." He had a worried look on his face, and said, "Ali, do you have any friends there?

What will you do in Teheran?" I told him that during my visits to the Embassy, they had assured me that I had ample opportunities in Teheran. He looked at Bhabhi, and she said," Ali is right." I called Javed and he invited me to his house for lunch the next day. At night when Zaffar and I were in our room, he said to me, "Yaar Ali, I am sorry I cannot do anything for you."

Everything was moving so fast, and my mind was working overtime. I sat down with Zaffar to finalize my plans. I explained to him that the day before I fly off to Bombay, I would get married to Susie secretly. And, when I finally settled down in Teheran, I would send for her. Zaffar said, "Poor Susie! How will she handle all this by herself... her mother's objection... and what if she stops her from leaving?" I told him I had thought of that. I said to him, "Zaffar, you and Rana will take her to the airport after she sneaks out of the house." No one can dare Rana, and Zaffar agreed.

I went to the travel agency and booked a flight to Bombay on PIA a week from the day of our plans. I called Susie and told her to meet me on the morrow. I went to the next-door neighbour of our meeting place. She was an Iranian divorcee, and a cousin of my friend, Abbas. I asked her for help; she knew about me and Susie, and after I explained to her about my plans, she said, "Ali, I will make arrangements for a maulvi - Muslim priest - to get you married on the date you have given me. You will get married in my house and I will be one of the witnesses. Don't worry, whatever is best for you will happen."

The next morning, I met Susie. And for the first time, I introduced her to Papoli, our Iranian neighbour. She assured Susie of her support. Papoli said, "Susie, after you get married and Ali leaves, every week, you must gradually bring some clothes and keep them with me. At the time of your departure, it'll be better if you leave from here."

When we were alone, I told her that Zaffar and Rana would take her from the house straight to the airport, and no one could stop her. I continued, "Susie, for God's sake, stop crying. You are making me nervous. Once you have joined me in Teheran, your parents will forgive you after a while."

A day before my departure, I went to Maritime to bid farewell to everyone. It was a very emotional moment - hugging everybody there, from Hassan the boxer to Mr. Khokar, and Hamid momoo, who had become a real mamoo to me. Surprisingly, Sanlay bahiya hugged me, too, and said, "Ali, go with our blessings and I know you will make a success of it. Who knows I will visit you one day " Afzalia took me aside and asked me if all was well with the tickets, and if I needed some cash. I said, "Afzalia, from the beginning you have done a lot for me and I will never forget you. No, I don't need any cash. I have some savings." He gave me a tight hug and said, "Go, Allah is with you."

The next morning, Susie came to our house and from there, we went to Papoli's to get hitched. The maulvi was to come at eleven a.m. but he did not show up. We were on pins and needles. Papoli said he must have been caught up in some other ceremony. It was two in the afternoon and there was still no news, so Papoli picked up the phone and called her friend who had arranged for this priest.

Her friend told her she would check and call back, and after one hour the bad and sad news arrived. The rickshaw that the priest was coming in had turned turtle after an accident, and he had landed in the hospital with a broken foot. What are the odds? What is God telling us? Maybe this is not the way....

Maybe we should get married only with parents' approval.

A hundred things were crossing our minds. We were confused. Finally, we decided that when I send for Susie from Teheran, she would go and tell her mum all about our love and affair, and our meetings in our hide out. Her mum would then agree, I was sure. With that settled, Susie and I stayed in our bubble, till Jani aunty, my ex-brother-in-law's mum came. I introduced Susie to her, and she said smiling, "So, this is the girl you have been seeing. She is very pretty!" And Susie left, taking my heart with her.

On my last night in Karachi, we all gathered in the living room after dinner. While having tea, we were reminiscing my first day, when I was adopted. Bhaiya said, "Ali, the last two months were the most grueling, especially editing. And, you handled it like a pro." He then handed me a certificate on Movie Makers letterhead, which said that I had handled both the assistant and the acting Production Managers' job professionally, and that he can safely recommend me for any such responsibility.

The kids went to sleep, but we sat and talked till two or three a.m. Everyone knew this was my last night, so no one wanted to get up. Amma and abba talked about our several trips to Hawks Bay, and there was so much to talk about. We wanted to keep holding on to the memories.

Finally, Bhaiya said, "Ali should rest so let's go to sleep."

In our room, Zaffar and I continued our plans, and we kept on going over them again and again to make sure that all goes smoothly. In the morning, after breakfast, Bhaiya said, "Ali, once you have settled down, I want you to come and visit us regularly." I said, "Allah willing." I hugged Shakila and Shakil, and then the others. And, then Zaffar took me to the airport.

On the way to the airport, I asked Zaffar if he could stop at Munna's house, which was my first home away from home. He said, "Sure, of course." I met amma, badi ommo, Munna, and the family. It's really hard to say goodbye, not knowing if you would ever get to meet them again. But something in my heart kept on whispering that I will see all of them again. All these family ties cannot just come to an end... never ever. And, I promised myself that God willing, I shall come again. My roots have been firmly grounded here.

On the way to the airport, I asked Zaffar to keep contact with Susie and make sure that she is okay, and that she should not fret. I said, "Tell her that I have assured you that by hook or by crook, I will send for her to join me in Teheran. All she has do is to be patient and have faith in God, for HE knows best."

When we arrived at the airport, Zaffar parked the van, and helped me with my luggage, which the coolie took over. I had bought from Bombay a small, tin trunk and a bed roll. I was leaving with a leather suitcase - given to me by Afzalia — and plenty of good clothes. Zaffar came up to the immigration booth, and that was the toughest final hug. I had tears in my eyes, and said, "Khuda Hafiz - God be with you."

Tram I used to take to work

Palace Hotel

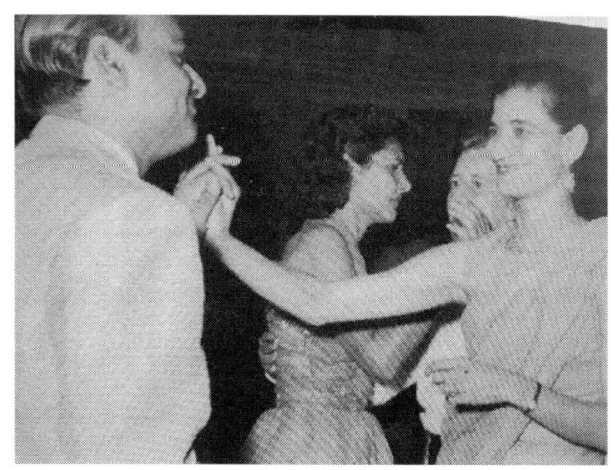

Afzalia and Bhbay

Bardi Bhbay

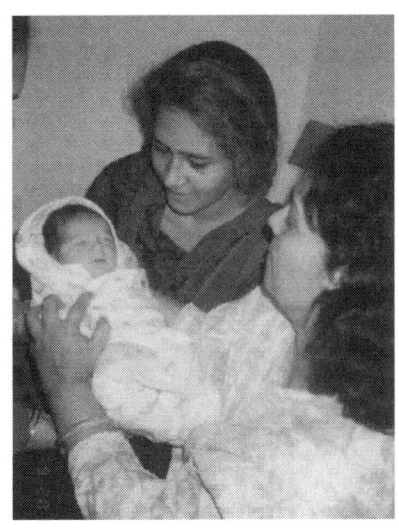

Chabbi, Bhbay and Baby

Dancing with Spanish Artist from Le Gourmmeh

Deborah, Suzie and Baby

Different Step Rock n Roll with Thelma and Sue

First time facing camera with Charlie in Sitaron Ki Duniya

Eddie semi-nude

George, Razi, Zaffar and Self drunk in Le Gourmet

Hamid Mamoo

Hawks Bay Abba, Amma and Bhabies

In Monkey Madari Garb

In our Love Nest

Iranian girlfriend, Nasreen

Le Gourmet Bhaiya Musti et al

Le Gourmet with actor Ejaz Durani

Le Gourmet - Imams and my girl Suzie

Little Totoo and Samina

Lunch with Ejaz, Suzie and Rakshi

Munna

Music Director Deebo Bhatchriya

My girl Dorothy, Can-Can Artist, Le Gourmet

Dorothy

Musti and Self

My girl Dorothy, Can-Can Artist, Le Gourmet

On Location – Self, Gilani, Rakshi and Charlie

On location with Mazhar Abba

Paragon Pictures, Meena, Bhaiya, Self and Chikoo

Rakshi

Portrait of Self

Rakshi

Rauf, my very first friend

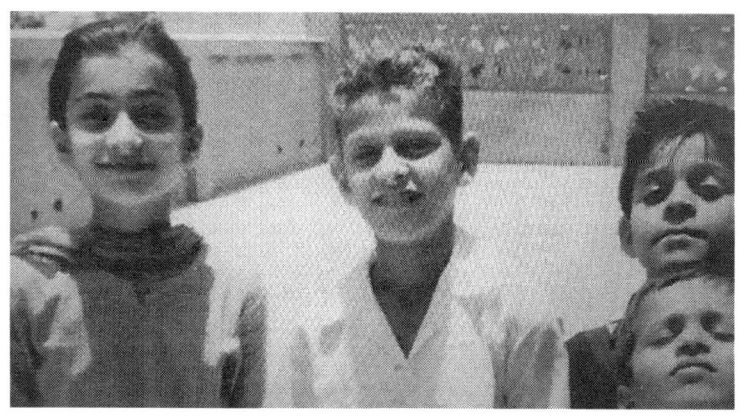

Samina, Shakil, Guddu and Tutoo

Hawks Bay with Sanley, Bahiya, Abba, Bardi,
Bhaby. Kids: Amma and Self

Sanley, Bahiys house family with Himalyawalla

Sanley, Baiyas House. Self, Bhiya and Afzalia

Self – 3 poses

Self as Prime Minister – On Set

Self – Karachi film magazine

Self on camel

Self on set

Self, Suzie and Mum in Le Gourmet

Shakil and Shakila on camel

Self with clapper board

Shakila and Raju

Shiro, Kido and self at lunch

Sitaron-Ki-Duniya Rock n Roll

Sitaron-Ki- Duniya Rock n Roll

Sitaron-Ki-Duniya Rock n Roll

Still photo of Rock n Roll

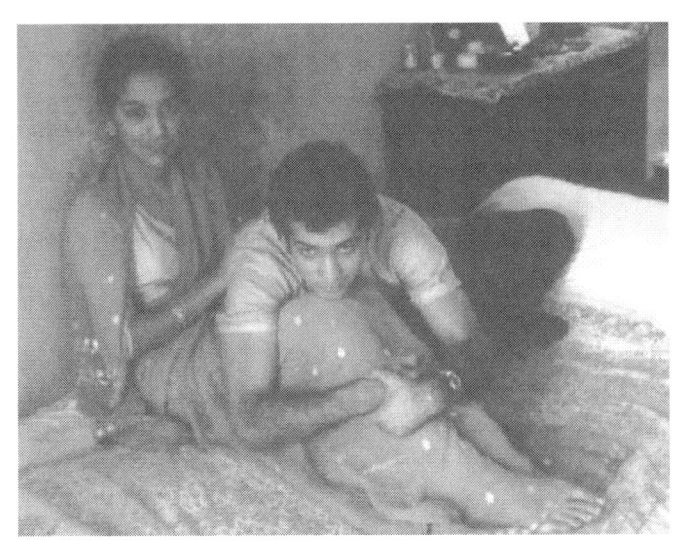

Sue and self in our Love nest

Sue in my thoughts montage

Sue in our Love Nest

Sue with candle

Sue and I dancing

Suzie black dhupaata

Suzie sad

Suzie sari

With Abba and Soli

With Irish girl Ann

On set with Chikoo

With Musti and Zaffar

With Zaffar on location

Yvonne and Self – Rock n Roll in film

Zaffar and Self

Zaffar and Self

Zaffar on camel

Zaffar, Yvonne and Susie on a picnic

Zaffar's first dance with Suzie

Printed in Great Britain
by Amazon